Talking, Listening, Learning

Talking, Listening, Learning

Effective Talk in the Primary Classroom

Debra Myhill, Susan Jones and Rosemary Hopper

Open University Press

Open University Press
McGraw-Hill Education
McGraw-Hill House
Shoppenhangers Road
Maidenhead
Berkshire
England
SL6 2QL

email: enquiries@openup.co.uk
world wide web: www.openup.co.uk

and Two Penn Plaza, New York, NY 10121-2289, USA

© Debra Myhill, Susan Jones and Rosemary Hopper 2006

A catalogue record of this book is available from the British Library

ISBN-10: 0 335 21744 3 (pb)   0 335 21745 1 (hb)
ISBN-13: 978 0335 21744 1 (pb)   978 0335 21745 8 (hb)

Library of Congress Cataloging-in-Publication Data
CIP data applied for

Typeset by RefineCatch Limited, Bungay, Suffolk
Printed in the UK by Bell and Bain Ltd, Glasgow

Contents

This is a book of many voices – the voices of researchers, teachers, headteachers and children. Although we have worked collaboratively in writing this book, you will hear our respective voices in different chapters. Debra Myhill was responsible for writing Chapters 1, 3 and 5; Susan Jones for Chapters 2, 4 and 6; and Rosemary Hopper wrote Chapter 7.

List of figures and tables

Preface

The story of the TALK project

As headteachers working in First Schools in West Sussex, we already had a passion and strong vision for a developmental approach to children's learning. But this passion was further fanned by Professor Charles Desforges in his keynote speeches to local headteachers at an in-service training day in the spring of 1999. This led to our realization that, in questioning the fundamental approaches being espoused within the national frameworks for literacy and numeracy, we were reaffirming our personal philosophy and belief systems about children's learning and development.

We had, through discussion, expressed gut reactions to the way that the whole class teaching episodes in the literacy and numeracy sessions seemed to be impacting on children's learning. We all had concerns that the children's learning was not being successfully scaffolded during these 'interactive' sessions, leading to a lack of true and deep understanding. Our concern was that teachers were beginning to understand that good teaching was the delivery of a prescribed model lesson – it appeared that good teaching no longer took into account children's learning. As part of a local schools' training network for teachers, we approached the University of Exeter for support in delivering the key message that the quality of learning was important.

Informal and formal opportunities for talk with the University of Exeter team led us to conceive the possibilities of testing our hypotheses in a structured and rigorous research project. The success of the bid left us speechless – we were amazed to have been given the opportunity to work on a national research project. Little did we realize at this stage that one of the most significant outcomes would be the involvement and professional development of the teachers in the classroom.

The impact on classroom practice and the learning environment

The impact on the teachers involved was one of the most striking outcomes of the TALK project. Initially the development of a booklet of guidance for teachers was seen as the way in which their practice would be developed. But in the event, the teachers involved moved from being passive research subjects to being active teacher-participants, including 10 of them subsequently engaging in Best Practice Research Scholarships, following up their own questions on aspects of the TALK project.

Their excitement and enthusiasm at the first meeting to launch the TALK project was palpable. From the beginning there was the attitude that this was important and that as they were chosen to be involved we, as headteachers and the research team from Exeter, believed in them and valued them as professionals. The TALK project was presented as relevant to them in terms of their teaching the National Literacy Strategy and the National Numeracy Strategy, and also as an opportunity to reflect within a structured framework on their own practice.

It was when the teachers watched their own teaching, following the videoing and observation of three of their teaching sessions, that their insights into their practice became evident. The video and the chance to reflect allowed them to explore critically their own practice. Reflecting on how they used talk as a tool for learning within the national strategies extended their understanding of the value, or otherwise, of whole class interactive teaching. Their analysis of how interactive teaching actually played out in their own classrooms was insightful and perceptive, and recognized their status as skilled professionals.

This sense of their own professionalism was reinforced by working collaboratively with their headteachers and with our researcher colleagues from the University of Exeter. This gave them a terrific boost as professional practitioners in their own schools – they were no longer just delivering the national strategies, they had the confidence to engage with them and change their own practice where necessary. It empowered them as they realized that they had a voice and that good teachers are not just curriculum deliverers but enablers, enabling children and themselves to take the initiative and become active questioning learners. As practitioners they have gained a voice and an eagerness to be involved with research, which has become a key part of their professional development.

The impact on the headteachers

We, the headteachers involved in the TALK project, discovered that our academic and professional status was valued by colleagues and other members of the profession, and indeed strengthened through our participation. We also found it increased our confidence in being able to draw on evidence-based research to articulate with a new-found vocabulary the practices and theoretical frameworks that characterize our schools. The research process and its subsequent findings gave us the evidence that in turn empowered us to change practices and pedagogical principles at grassroots level.

The direct and independent relationship with the University of Exeter, without the indirect influences from the government or local education authority, was a genuine strength of the project. It allowed us to engage in rigorous and challenging academic dialogue directly linked to real practice in the classrooms. It was a real opportunity for us to raise our own thinking and learning above the day-to-day running of the school to become leading learners in a learning community.

We were also given opportunities rarely afforded to headteachers, that of presenting to wider academic audiences both at the British Educational Research Association annual conference in Exeter in 2002 and subsequently at the European Association of Research in Learning and Instruction in Padua in 2003. These conferences enabled us to engage with and learn from fellow professionals from the national and international learning communities.

The Economic and Social Research Council awarded the project significant but realistic funding which enabled us to have both the time and space to be reflective learners and thus influence practice in our own schools. If school-based research projects are to be successful both in their influence on children's learning and the development of pedagogy, and to be supported by governors, then schools must be given the necessary funding that will benefit them, not disadvantage them financially.

TALK enabled us and our teachers to truly develop pedagogical practice in order to improve children's learning experiences in schools. Without a doubt, this has raised standards and influenced school improvement in our own school communities.

Margaret Brackley – Headteacher: Thomas A'Becket
First School, Worthing
Frances Dunkin – Headteacher: Field Place First School, Worthing
Pauline Warren – Headteacher: Elm Grove First school, Worthing

Introduction

The status of talk in English classrooms is an ambivalent one. On one hand, talk has more official recognition now than at any time in our educational history; on the other hand, as a culture we value reading and writing more highly than oral competence and our assessment system is still conducted predominantly in the written mode. In the pre-GCSE era, there existed a deficit model of oracy, which suggested that it was a way of compensating for the lack of writing ability in lower achieving pupils: O-levels were assessed wholly through writing, but the Certificate of Secondary Education (CSE), a lower level academic award, made use of an oral examination, as well as a written one. By including speaking and listening as a Programme of Study in the first version of the National Curriculum for English (DES 1990) oracy, for the first time, was given a status parallel to that of reading and writing. However, the introduction of the National Literacy Strategy in 1998 appeared to sideline the place of pupil talk in the primary curriculum. First, it offered a definition of literacy which seemed unsure about the role of talk: it initially defined literacy as being essentially about reading and writing, but continued to assert the role of talk in achieving this:

> Literacy unites the important skills of reading and writing. It also involves speaking and listening which, although they are not separately identified in the Framework, are an essential part of it. Good oral work enhances pupils' understanding of language in both oral and written forms and of the way language can be used to communicate. It is also an important part of the process through which pupils read and compose texts.
>
> (DfEE 1998: 3)

Second, as the extract above indicates, it did not include speaking and listening in the teaching objectives set out in the Framework. In contrast, the Framework for English at Key Stage 3 (DfEE 2001) has a specific set of objectives under the heading of Speaking and Listening.

Whilst many of these objectives address the National Curriculum goal of improving children's competence in speaking and listening, some of these objectives are explicitly about teachers supporting children in using talk for learning and thinking. The following list of objectives are taken from the Speaking and Listening objectives in years, 7, 8 and 9 in section 2 of the Framework:

- use talk as a tool for clarifying ideas;
- use exploratory, hypothetical and speculative talk as a way of researching ideas and expanding thinking;
- work together logically and methodically to solve problems, make deductions, share, test and evaluate ideas;
- ask questions to clarify understanding and refine ideas;
- use talk to question, hypothesize, speculate, evaluate, solve problems, and develop thinking about complex issues and ideas;
- recognize and build on other people's contributions;
- contribute to the organization of group activity in ways that help to structure plans, solve problems and evaluate alternatives.

(DfEE 2001: section 2, 23–32)

More recently, there has been significant and constructive attention given to talk in the curriculum by the Qualifications and Curriculum Authority (QCA). Three publications in particular explicitly support the development of a stronger place for talk in the classroom. As part of the Primary National Strategy, a pack of guidance materials, *Speaking, Listening, Learning* (DfES 2003) has been produced for teachers. The inclusion of the word 'learning' in the title is a reminder that the pack focuses not just on teaching oral competence but also upon the role of talk in enhancing learning. It includes a set of teaching objectives (perhaps to compensate for missing them out first time round!), a teacher's handbook, and guidance on how to foster effective speaking, listening, group inter-action and drama. The teacher's handbook underlines the recognition of the symbiotic relationship between language and learning, and the particular role of talk within this. The opening sentence states that 'language is an integral part of most learning and oral language in particular has a key role in classroom teaching and learning. Children's creativity, understanding and imagination can be engaged and fostered by discussion and interaction' (DfES 2003: 3). For secondary teachers, where speaking and listening are already more formally part of the curriculum, the publication *Introducing the Grammar of Talk* (QCA 2004) considers how grammatical and linguistic insights can enhance secondary students' understanding of how talk works. The third publication, *New Perspectives on Spoken English in the Classroom* (QCA 2003), is particularly relevant to this book as it addresses most directly the relationship between talking and learning, and the pedagogical implications of changing class-room practice to create stronger talk-for-learning environments. Several articles in this book build on an earlier seminar held by QCA, stimulated by a keynote speech by Robin Alexander, which looked at 'the nature of spoken exchanges between teachers and pupils, contrasting the short question and response sequences typical of English classrooms with models in other countries where pupils were encouraged to speak more extensively, explaining their ideas to the whole class' (QCA 2003: 3).

The contrast in the role of talk for learning between English and American classrooms on the one hand, and many other European classrooms, is described in detail by Alexander (2002) in his compara-tive study of the relationship between culture and classroom practices across the world. Alexander draws contrasts between English and European pedagogies which are significant to the thrust of this book. Whole class teaching as a pedagogic strategy is more common in European classrooms, but it is not the kind of whole class teaching that is familiar in England. In England, children talk to the teacher and wait their turn (or carefully avoid a turn), whereas in Russia, for example, children talk to the rest of the class. The talk and learning is much more public and collective. This public–private distinction is important. In England the more public arena of whole class teaching tends to focus on correctness and right answers and teachers are anxious not to expose or humiliate children by drawing attention to errors. English teachers are more likely to have private one-to-one conversations with children individually to talk about errors or mis-understandings. In contrast, Russian children will bring problems they are having to the rest of the class and everyone will join in trying to seek clarification or understanding. Whereas talk in England is often conceptualized in terms of its social function, European class-rooms conceptualize talk in terms of a cognitive function, though achieved through social interaction.

Alexander notes that the surface features of talk which appear to characterize a classroom culture often belie its true purposes. He observes that talk in English and American classrooms may appear to be dialogue, but is not genuinely so because it is not directed with sufficient clarity to children's learning, and is often more concerned with social engagement and participation. Perhaps rather harshly, he describes English classroom talk as 'warm, determinedly inclusive, engaging but cognitively undemanding; and which prefers habitual, bland and eventually phatic praise to focused feedback, for fear that children might be discouraged by the latter' (QCA 2003: 33). In contrast, French classrooms may appear casually conversational but are actually strongly controlled by the teacher towards developing understanding of an educational goal.

What is clear is that the challenge of making whole class teaching an effective context for learning is not an easy one, and that our social and cultural values may influence the practices and activities we attempt to introduce into the classroom. The emphasis on whole class teaching in the National Primary Strategy derives not from European models of primary education, but from the Far East and the perceived correlation between whole class teaching and high attainment. There has been considerable criticism of this return to whole class teaching, with all its cultural associations of transmission, didacticism and heavy teacher control. Critics have argued that the combination of high stakes testing and accountability, Ofsted inspection, and the scale of the curriculum coverage required means that whole class teaching is less than effective: 'with a great deal to get through, the pace of transmission is likely to be fast. This privileges the teacher's talk, producing not only a great deal of exposition but also a pre-dominance of questions to which the answers are likely to be short and readily 'marked' (Edwards 2003: 39). But teachers are profes-sionals and agents of change in their own right, capable of reflective thought and thoughtful action. This book celebrates one group of teachers who took up this challenge.

The research underpinning this book, conducted in collaboration with a cluster of primary schools in Worthing, was given an apt quasi-acronym, the TALK project (Teaching and Learning to Activate children's Knowledge). How the TALK project began, was sub-sequently developed, and how it engaged teachers, headteachers and researchers in reflection on practice is outlined in more detail in Chapter 2. But we hope this book will stimulate your reflection upon the most effective ways for teachers to create classrooms where talk is a tool for learning and thinking, and where teachers' interactions with children generate responses which are exploratory, open and purposeful. At times, this book is critical of national policy initiatives; at times, it is critical of some teachers' practice; at all times, it is mindful of the limitations of the researcher, but it is our hope that the book is not read as a critique or an endorsement of anything or anyone. Rather it is an acknowledgement of the professional commitment and capacity of the educational establishment. Working in partnership with teachers to investigate classroom practice has been a privilege and we hope this book will convey some of that spirit of shared and evolving understanding. Throughout the chapters that draw on the TALK project we have included three different invitations to you as reader to engage with this process of shared reflection upon practice: 'Talking point'; 'Teachers' voices'; and a 'Spotlight on Good Practice'. In the Talking point sections, we raise some questions which you could use as a school or staff subgroup to prompt thinking about how talk is used in your classrooms. The Teachers' voices sections articulate the perspectives of the teachers involved in the study and you could consider how these chime with your own viewpoints or with the realities of teaching in your school. Finally, the Spotlight on Good Practice highlights teaching strategies which the teachers successfully used to improve the quality of the talking, listening and thinking experiences of the children in their classes. They are not 'Tips for Teachers'; they are not formulaic recipes for success; and we invite you to use and adapt them to suit the needs of the children you teach, and to experiment and create new ideas of your own.

In Chapter 1 we outline the theoretical basis for the TALK project, and review the national and international research on talking and learning. Chapter 2 suggests ways that you can investigate talk in your own classrooms, drawing on the tools and techniques that we used. As interaction is at the heart of this book, Chapter 3 sets out some of the issues surrounding the concept of interactive teaching and presents some of the patterns of interaction found in the classrooms in our study. Chapter 4 takes a fresh look at teachers' questions: it considers the weakness of simplistic classifications of questions as open or closed and offers an alternative way of thinking about questions in terms of their form and function. In Chapter 5, we consider how teachers use children's prior knowledge as a starting-point or building-block for introducing new learning. Many teaching episodes create critical moments, those moments where the teacher's on-the-spot decision about how to handle a particular response or situation is critical in determining the quality of what ensues, and in Chapter 6 we examine some of those critical moments in whole class teaching. The focus of Chapter 7 is capturing the teachers' experiences of being involved in this research and how they changed, or found it difficult to change their own classroom practice. Finally, in the Conclusion we will consider the implications for policy and practice that emerge from this study.

Although this book records and explores the experiences of one particular group of teachers, we hope that we have presented this in a manner which encourages you to co-participate in some of the thinking, collaboration and reflection that characterized the TALK study.

psychological theories of how children learn that were dominant at the time but which retain their currency today. In particular it reflects the shift from Piagetian to Vygotskian theories of learning and with it a parallel shift from the importance of action to the importance of language. Piaget believed that children learned through action and that learning was thus a process of discovery in which children could not progress to higher levels until they were ready. The role of language in Piaget's thinking was secondary to action: thought derived from action, and language was simply the medium of expression of that understanding. Vygotsky (1986) however believed that language is central to learning and the interrelationship between thinking; talking and learning is paramount. For Vygotsky, the process of verbalizing gives substance to thinking; as Corden puts it, 'thought is not merely expressed in words – it comes into existence through words' (2000: 7). Through talking, we can *formulate* ideas for the first time, crystallizing inner thoughts into substance and shaping our ideas into existence; we can *reformulate* our ideas so that our thinking and understanding is clarified, focused or modified; we can *communicate* our ideas with other people through interaction and feedback; and we can *reflect* upon our learning through talk (Howe 1992).

For the primary school teacher especially, the move from Piagetian ways of thinking about teaching to those of Vygotsky represented a significant alteration in the role of the teacher. Piaget believed in age-related developmental stages, whereas Vygotsky believed that language was the crucial factor. Piaget believed teachers should not teach anything until children were ready for it, whereas Vygotsky believed teachers should help children progress by moving them on one stage from where they were to help them understand or do something they could not previously do. Edwards and Mercer (1987: 170) describe this distinction in two apt metaphors: Piaget would encourage children to learn in a 'discovery sandpit', whereas Vygotsky would prompt children to tackle a 'cognitive climbing frame'. Therefore, unlike Piaget, Vygotsky believed in the value of instruction, and learning as a social communicative process. His concept of the Zone of Proximal Development (ZPD) represents the relationship of the learner with the teacher as one where a novice is supported by an expert in learning with assistance or support until the learning is mastered and becomes independent of support. What the individual is capable of achieving is increased if careful cognitive assistance is provided, and good teaching always challenges the learner to tackle things they have not yet fully mastered. In Vygotsky's terms, 'What the child can do in co-operation today, he can do alone tomorrow. Therefore the only good kind of instruction is that which marches ahead of development and leads it: it must be aimed not so much at the ripe as at the ripening functions' (1986: 188).

With the emphasis on learning as a social communicative process developed through interaction with peers and with experts, the role of the teacher in establishing and managing interactions which promote social, collaborative learning through talk is a complex one. Teacher talk, rather than simply transmitting learning to children, is fundamental to the process of co-constructing understanding and needs to provide cognitive assistance and challenge at an appropriate level for children to progress.

Scaffolding learning through interaction

The first application of the word 'scaffolding' to an educational context is attributed to Bruner (1978) who observed the way parents interact with their children to help them learn. He noted how initially parents would offer high degrees of support, but would gradually withdraw the support until the child could perform the task independently. This observation was developed in subsequent research studies. Wells (1986) explored in depth how parents and children used talk and his transcripts of home conversations show parents extending children's thinking by making deliberate attempts to understand what the child is attempting to communicate, and how their responses make effective use of paraphrasing, introduce new words, and respond spontaneously to opportunities as they arise. In borrowing the word 'scaffolding' to describe this process, Bruner draws attention to knowledge creation as a joint, social achievement, where the role of the 'expert' operates within a particular framework of support. Of course, for the teacher, scaffolding learning in the classroom is not the same as for the parent in the home. Wells observed that parent–child interactions were frequently more supportive and developmental than those found in teacher–child conversations in the classroom. Teachers were only able to 'incorporate the meanings offered in the children's utterances, either by extending those meanings or by inviting children to extend them themselves' half as often as parents did (Wells 1986: 87). Mercer (1995) distinguishes clearly between the role of the teacher and the role of the parent in these conversations: first the objective of the teacher's interactions is explicitly learning, and second the teacher is not usually in a one-to-one ratio with the child in the classroom.

Nonetheless, the concept of scaffolding children's learning has become a common way of describing learning relationships in the classroom. Indeed, some of the pedagogic strategies advocated by the National Literacy and Numeracy Strategies such as demonstration, modelling, and shared writing are clearly linked to principles of scaffolding. However there is a growing tendency to use the word 'scaffolding' synonymously with 'support' without examining precisely what is meant by scaffolding in an educational setting. When working with PGCE students, we often introduce the idea of scaffolding by asking students first to brainstorm individually all the words and ideas they associate with the word 'scaffold' and then in groups to cluster the ideas into associated concepts. Finally, we collate a concept map of the word 'scaffold', which is then used as the basis for discussion of educational scaffolding. (To date, no one has ever linked the word to a pop group of the 60s! Surprisingly, it is also rare for anyone to think of the hangman's scaffold, which does not link well to the educational concept.) Figure 1.1 presents one example of one of these concept maps.

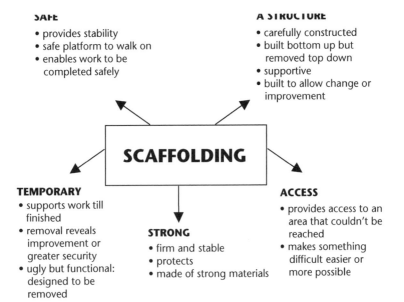

Figure 1.1 Scaffolding concept map

One way to consider what scaffolding means in the classroom, and thus how talk might best be used to scaffold children's learning, is to think of scaffolding as possessing four important qualities.

1 *Scaffolding occurs with assistance.*
The key principle of scaffolding is that the learner is supported by someone more experienced, usually a teacher but possibly a peer, in order to acquire new knowledge, a new skill or a new understanding:

> When social interactions in a classroom focus on content or strategies within a learner's zone of proximal development, a teacher or more able peer supplies scaffolding for the novice learner. Such scaffolding provides the support or assistance that enables learners to develop understandings or use strategies they would not have been capable of independently.
>
> (Many 2002: 376)

The assistance is carefully designed to challenge learners to move beyond what they can already do, effectively drawing on the greater knowledge of their peer or teacher. In this way 'teachers lend their mental capacities to learners in order to support and shape learning' (Goodwin 2001: 129).

2 *Scaffolding is focused.*
Effective scaffolding focuses the learner on a particular skill or aspect of understanding and limits 'the degree of freedom in carrying out some task so that the child can concentrate on the difficult skill she is in the process of acquiring' (Bruner 1978: 19). So, for example, rather than modelling how to write a persuasive argument, a teacher might model how to shape the opening paragraph only; or in developing confidence in understanding multiplication or division by three, the teacher might set up a card sort activity which only has numbers that are multiples of three and multiples of two, rather than using a genuinely more random set of numbers.

3 *Scaffolding avoids failure.*
A further feature of scaffolding is that it 'reduces the learner's scope for failure in the task' (Mercer 2000: 139) in the way that the task is designed. An obvious example of this is the use of

stabilizers on a bike when a child is first learning to ride. A more classroom-oriented example might be shared writing, where the teacher and the class co-author a piece of writing.

4 *Scaffolding is temporary.*
Finally, the process of scaffolding should not be a permanent support structure. Effective scaffolding considers not only how to support but how that support might be removed to help the learner become independent. As Maybin *et al.* (1992: 186) explain, scaffolding describes the 'temporary, but essential, nature of the mentor's assistance as the learner advances in knowledge and understanding'.

This final quality of scaffolding, its temporariness, is particularly important as there have been concerns that the way scaffolding is actually used in the classroom focuses too much on support and not enough on how to withdraw that support. Writing frames give very strong support for shaping a piece of writing but if young writers are never given encouragement to move away from the writing frame, it becomes a straitjacket, not a support, and is not developing learning. Edwards and Mercer (1987) call the point of withdrawal of support the 'handover to independence' and argue that it rarely happens, meaning that scaffolding fosters dependence rather than independence.

David Wray, drawing on the work of Vygotsky and Palincsar and Brown (1984) provides a very clear account of scaffolding and how the child is helped in moving from a point of considerable dependence to one of independence.

> Children first experience a particular cognitive activity in collaboration with expert practitioners. The child is firstly a spectator as the majority of the cognitive work is done by the expert (parent or teacher), then a novice as he/she starts to take over some of the work under the close supervision of the expert. As the child grows in experience and capability of performing the task, the expert passes over greater and greater responsibility but still acts as a guide, assisting the child at problematic points. Eventually, the child assumes full responsibility for the task with the expert still present in the role of a supportive audience.
>
> (www.warwick.ac.uk/staff/D.J.Wray/Articles/teach.html)

Translating this to the classroom, Wray and Lewis ascribe a particular role to the teacher for each of the four stages described above. They term the four stages demonstration, joint activity, supported activity, and independence. Another way of considering scaffolding is to see it as an apprenticeship in thinking, as Barbara Rogoff (1991) does, and to see the joint role of the teacher and the learner as one that fosters guided participation through helping children to adapt their understanding to new situations, structuring their problem-solving attempts, and assisting them in assuming responsibility for managing problem-solving (Rogoff 1991: 191). In terms of whole class teaching and how teachers use talk to scaffold children's learning, the idea of guided participation seems particularly apt, as the teacher has to simultaneously guide the thinking and understanding of the class and ensure the fullest participation possible. Alexander (2002: 436) argues that the principal way of scaffolding children's understanding is through what he calls 'guided discovery', although he questions whether what actually happens in the classroom is genuinely discovery, as it is characterized by heavy prompts, clues and cues, and thus is rather more like direct instruction.

Interaction patterns in teacher–pupil talk

The talk that occurs between teacher and children, especially during whole class teaching, is not like conversation; the teacher has a clear purpose and intention for conducting the talk, and although the talk itself is rarely planned, neither is it entirely spontaneous. The discourse pattern is one in which 'the possibilities for subordinate participants are severely limited' (Cook 1989: 50) and one for which children learn the rules in their first few years at school (Sinclair and Coulthard 1975). Edwards and Mercer highlight not only the existence of these 'educational ground rules' for classroom talk, but note a further level of complexity – there are different rules with different subjects and different teachers (1987: 48). Alexander (2002: 526) identifies that across many countries there are three predominant patterns of teacher talk: rote, which involves 'the drilling of facts, ideas and routines through constant repetition'; recitation, which involves strong cueing of answers and 'the accumulation of knowledge and understanding through questions designed to test or stimulate recall of what has been encountered previously'; and instruction/exposition which is more directive, involving 'telling the pupil what to do, and/or imparting information, and/or explaining facts, principles or procedures'.

Many descriptions of the teacher's role in classroom discourse create the image of teacher as an orchestrator of the interactions, conducting the responses from the class, signalling who should contribute, and controlling the outcomes. The Bullock Report uses this image explicitly, suggesting that a lesson should be 'a verbal encounter through which the teacher draws information from the class, elaborates and generalises it, and produces a synthesis. His skill is in selecting, prompting, improving, and generally orchestrating the exchange' (DES 1975: 141). Observing teacher talk in orderly class-rooms, Edwards and Westgate (1994) found interaction patterns where the teacher played the role advocated by Bullock. In leading whole class teaching, the teacher 'takes turns at will, allocates turns to others, determines topics, interrupts and re-allocates turns judged to be irrelevant to those topics, and provides a running commentary on what is being said and meant which is the main source of cohesion within and between the various sequences of the lesson' (Edwards and Westgate 1994: 46).

Not surprisingly, this orchestration of talk can result in consider-able asymmetry in contributions to the classroom talk. Some of this imbalance is due to the different status and authority of the teacher, and the professional responsibilities of ensuring that the classroom is a place where learning can happen. However, it does mean that the teacher talks a lot more than the children. The first ORACLE project in 1976–8 observed this 'asymmetry of the interaction process in the primary classroom' (Galton *et al.* 1999: 23). The teacher spent 78 per cent of the time interacting with children, but an individual child spent 84 per cent of time working on his/her own. Children received most teacher attention during whole class teaching and there were greater levels of on-taskness. In group activity, 60 per cent of the time was off-task talk. Research like this, which indicated that, contrary to popular belief, whole class teaching gave children more attention, rather than less, was part of the stimulus to move to increased levels of whole class teaching in the National Literacy and Numeracy Strategies. However contrary perspectives on the interaction patterns constructed by whole class teaching suggest that children are cast in 'the primary role of listeners' not speakers, and that in most cases whole class discussion was in fact small group discussion with the rest of the class listening in (Bousted 1989: 42). The ORACLE follow-up study in 1996, which of course predates the introduction of the

National Strategies, argued that the National Curriculum had altered interaction patterns so that primary classrooms were more like secondary classrooms where 'teachers talk and pupils sit and listen' (Galton *et al.* 1999: 34).

Asymmetric discourse where the children are positioned to listen to the teacher and offer contributions when invited is frequently played out through an interaction pattern commonly described as the IRF pattern. The teacher Initiates a spoken sequence, a child Responds, and the teacher provides Feedback, then moves on to the next IRF sequence. The IRF pattern was described as the prototypical pattern of classroom discourse by Sinclair and Coulthard (1975). Clearly the IRF sequence creates asymmetry because the teacher automatically occupies two-thirds of the turns in any sequence, and all the children in the class have to share their one-third opportunity to contribute. The 'recitation script' described by Goodwin (2001: 11) is very similar and gives the teacher dominant air time: The teacher selects pupil speakers: there is little or no acknowledgement of pupil self-selection; pupil responses tend to be short, and the teacher does not encourage elaboration of responses; and the teacher uses many 'test' questions where the implied role of the pupil is to contribute a pre-determined 'right' answer in response. Alexander (2003: 32) argues that these typical patterns of interaction are neither conversation nor dialogue, and summarizes the characteristics of this form of interaction as:

- interactions tend to be brief rather than sustained;
- teachers ask questions about content, but children may ask questions only about points of procedure;
- closed questions predominate;
- children concentrate on identifying 'correct' answers;
- there is little speculative talk or 'thinking aloud';
- the child's answer marks the end of an exchange and the teacher's feedback formally closes it.

Not all classroom discourse conforms to this pattern, however, and some teachers demonstrate that it is possible to break the traditional asymmetries and create more learning-productive talk. Hughes and Westgate (1998) report a study that sets out to explore whether it is possible to identify moves or enabling strategies which teachers can use to foster better quality pupil talking and thinking.

The teacher studied did not use the Initiate–Respond–Feedback discourse sequence – she did not act as evaluator of their answers, but instead supported and built on their knowledge. She frequently agreed, praised, named children and referred back to things children had already said. The ratio of pupil turns to teacher turns was much higher than usual: children had twice as many turns as the teacher. Most importantly, 'the teacher appears to use her pupils' knowledge as a starting-point; she then either extends it or encourages children to extend it for themselves' (Hughes and Westgate 1998: 184).

The quality of teacher interactions with children

Clearly, by avoiding the conventional IRF interaction pattern, the teacher in Hughes and Westgate's study created a high quality interactive relationship between herself and the children. Several recent studies have looked at the quality of teacher interactions with learners in the context of recent initiatives, particularly the Literacy Hour in the UK. Mroz *et al.* (2000) observed and analysed 10 teachers' interactions with children in the literacy hour. They argue that, despite the NLS endorsement of interactive whole class teaching, there are still few opportunities for pupils to question or explore ideas. The requirement for predetermined outcomes and a fast pace seem to militate against reflection and exploration of ideas. Similarly, Moyles *et al.* (2001) showed that task-focused interactions and rapid-fire closed questions had increased in line with the NLS aims to promote well-paced whole class teaching. More positively, they did find that there was an increase in higher order interactions involving reasoning with 7–11-year-olds, but this was matched by a heavy emphasis on factual recall with the younger children.

Using two taped interaction sequences derived from guided reading sessions in the primary school, Skidmore (2000) compares one teacher who controls the learning in an authoritative style through her use of the IRF sequence with another teacher whose interactions promote more open-ended thinking and response to the text. This teacher does not adopt the IRF strategy but instead asks questions that act as genuine invitations to the children to articulate their views, and she hands over control of the conversation to the children. As a result, the teacher's contributions are much fewer than in conventional classroom dialogue and all the pupils make several contributions.

In the context of American classrooms, Many (2002) examined interactions between teachers and students, and between peers as they worked together to respond to literary and non-fiction texts. Unlike many US classrooms with traditional classroom interaction patterns, these teachers had established classroom environments that were essentially socioconstructivist in nature, and where learning was viewed as a joint endeavour. The analysis of the interactions showed that moments of scaffolding were woven through the conversations, supporting learners' conceptual understanding and the development of strategies for learning. Many argues that scaffolded instruction underscores both the role of the teacher and the role of the child as 'co-participants in negotiating meaning and in informing the nature of the instructional conversations' (Many 2002: 379).

Genuinely constructive interaction patterns such as those described by Hughes and Westgate, and Skidmore, challenge traditional teaching approaches, which still retain a strong presence in some classrooms, and are predicated on a view of teaching as an act of transmission, and the teacher as 'the self-effacing transmitter of the received wisdom' (Hodge and Malcolm 1981: 12). Transmission teaching conceptualizes talk merely as a mechanism for information transfer, yet contemporary learning theory asserts the impossibility of this: 'however unequal the balance of knowledge between teacher and learner, there is no way in which the knowledge of the teacher can be transmitted directly to the learner' (Wells 1986: 101). In contrast, the teacher in Hughes and Westgate's study used talking and listening as an opportunity to create understanding, rather than to transmit it. She had developed an interaction pattern which became 'a collaborative endeavour in which meanings are negotiated and some common knowledge is mobilized' (Mercer 2000: 6).

Teachers' questions

Whole class teaching draws heavily on the teacher's skill in questioning, as questioning remains the most common strategy for eliciting responses from children during a whole class teaching episode. Questioning in school is a very particular kind of questioning, however. Unlike most social contexts where you ask questions in order to establish something you don't know, teachers predominantly ask questions they know the answers to – and children know that there is usually a right answer to a teacher's question. There have been many studies of teachers' questions over the past 30 years, many of them arriving at the same conclusion: most questions have a single acceptable response and the principal goal for the child is to work out what answer is in the teacher's head.

Barnes' seminal analysis of teacher questioning (Barnes *et al.* 1986) categorized teachers' questions into four broad types: factual questions, which had a single right answer; reasoning questions, which drew on logical or sequential thought; open questions, to which there was no anticipated right answer; and social questions, which invited children to share their experiences or allowed the teacher to control the class. They found that factual questions were the most common and open questions the least common. The two studies conducted by the ORACLE project in 1976 and 1996 came to similar conclusions, finding that closed and factual questions predominated. The ORACLE project usefully distinguishes between teacher inter-actions with individuals or groups and whole class teaching, and observed that whilst the individual or group interactions were characterized by statements from the teacher, whole class teaching made much greater use of questions.

Implicit in the distinction made between open and closed questions is an assumption that open questions are good and closed questions are bad. Allerton's (1993) study of how children respond differently to open and closed question typifies this stance. He used a rather artificial methodology of asking one group of children only open questions and another group only closed questions, and found that the responses to open questions were longer and more divergent than responses to closed questions. His conclusions assert the superior value of open-ended questions, and he notes that 'open questions allow more insight into the way children think' (Allerton 1993: 47). Edwards and Mercer (1987) offer a challenge to this assumption, asking why there is always higher value attributed to open, inferential questions. Factual, closed questions which recall information may have more value than is acknowledged. Likewise, simply asking more open questions will not necessarily change the quality of children's thinking if they still think there is a right answer. Adopting a simplistic view that open questions are always preferable to closed questions may miss some of the different ways in which ques-tions can be used, and an effective questioning sequence might, for example, begin with a quick burst of closed recap questions to bring the topic to the foreground of children's thinking, followed by some reasoning questions, and conclude with an open question, or some questions that invite children to reflect on their thinking. It may be more appropriate to think about the right question at the right time.

One association frequently made between teachers' questioning, especially closed questions, and the quality of learning occurring in the classroom is that teachers' questions are frequently used as a controlling mechanism. Allerton (1993: 48) argues that where teaching is strongly directed towards curriculum goals, closed questioning may predominate 'because it allows the teacher to retain control of interactions'. In a study looking at teachers' interactions with children when sharing a story text, Kirby (1996) also identified a pattern of questioning being used to control. The teacher used questioning to lead children to her interpretation of the text, and to redirect them back from their own responses and meaning-making. In this interactional context, 'questions which required the children to extend their thinking or which sought to clarify the text meaning were rare' (Kirby 1996: 10). The National Literacy and Numeracy Strategies have emphasized the importance of teaching objectives and in outlining objectives for each term of each year of the primary school; curriculum coverage has also been foregrounded. A consequence of this is that primary teaching is often much more consciously focused upon specific learning outcomes than in the past. Whilst this may have made teaching more purposeful, it may also have fostered greater use of closed or factual questioning. Similarly, where teachers lack confidence in the subject knowledge underpinning a given topic, they may adopt a questioning style that allows them to retain control and avoid opening up issues or questions which they feel unable to answer. Watts *et al.* (1997: 1030) observed this in primary science lessons, where some of the teachers 'carefully formulate their planning, organization, assessment and materials and more tightly manage and control learning situations to minimize "exposure" of their own limited expertise'.

Where the relationship between control and questioning is close, the effect on interaction can be to produce passive, compliant or non-participative children. At its simplest, this is because the balance of power lies with the teacher as questioner and children are positioned to supply the answer, so that the questioning can continue. There is no room, as Dillon (1988) noted, for children to interrupt the cycle and insert their own question. Put bluntly, the more questions teachers ask, the less children say. Wood (1988: 143) argued that 'frequent specific questions tend to generate relatively silent children and to inhibit any discussion between them'. Much more recently, in the context of literacy teaching, Hargreaves *et al.* (2002) found that, in line with the NLS advocacy of pacy, interactive teaching, teachers had increased the number of questions they asked but children made very short responses averaging no more than three words. The consequences on learning of the attempt to manage a pacy, interactive teaching session are described by Black and Wiliam (1998: 8):

> There are then two consequences. One is that, because the only questions that can produce answers in such a short time are questions of fact, these predominate. The other is that pupils don't even try to think out a response – if you know the answer, or another question, will come along in a few seconds, there is no point in trying. It is also common that only a few pupils in a class answer teachers' questions. The rest then leave it to these few, knowing that they cannot respond as quickly and being unwilling to risk making mistakes in public. So the teacher, by lowering the level of questions and by accepting answers from a few, can keep the lesson going but is actually out of touch with the understanding of most of the class – the question–answer dialogue becomes a ritual, one in which all connive and thoughtful involvement suffers.

So what does effective questioning look like? Socrates, in his teaching relationship with his pupils, believed that questions should be primarily about stimulating the thinking processes of the learner, and that good questions 'promote reflection, analysis, self-examination and enquiry' (Wood 1988: 205). In other words, the directionality of teacher questioning should be wholly focused upon the quality of thinking the questions generate for the learner, rather than a teacher-centred directionality which uses questioning to elicit answers in the teacher's head. Wragg and Brown (2001a) suggest that to establish this more purposeful kind of questioning teachers need to rely less on spontaneous questioning and may instead need to think more carefully and prepare key questions in advance. Teachers' success in altering how they use whole class questions is evident in the collaborative research of the King's College Assessment for Learning team (Black *et al.* 2002). By changing the nature of questions asked, by making greater use of strategies such as pair work, and by extending the wait time given before taking responses, the teachers involved were better able to determine what children had understood or misunderstood and were better equipped to meet learners' needs. Correspondingly, children became 'more active as participants' and began to appreciate that good learning 'may depend less on their capacity to spot the right answer and more on their readiness to express and discuss their own understanding' (Black *et al.* 2002: 7).

Teachers' talk and use of children's prior knowledge

Increasing the effectiveness of children's participation in whole class teaching through better use of questioning enables children to become more involved in their own learning. The more each child is aware of his or her own understanding or uncertainties and the more he or she is encouraged to express those understandings, the better the classroom is as a community of learners who can see the interrelationships and connections between what they know and understand. One important function of teachers' talk in the classroom is to help make those connections between the learner's prior knowledge and the new learning to be addressed in the lesson.

One helpful way of thinking about prior knowledge is to draw on schema theory and its representation of learning in terms of schemata. Schema theory identifies prior knowledge as a fundamental contributor to the creation of new learning, and helps to articulate the relationships between established understanding and new understanding. Bartlett developed the first outline of schema theory in 1932, with a particular focus on the role of memory. He argued that memory is an active process, not reproductive, but constructive in its operation: when we encounter something new our understanding is shaped by what we already know. The schema is the 'mental map' or set of mental connections we hold in our heads about a particular idea or thing. Cook (1989) defines schemata as 'mental representations of typical situations', and similarly Kellogg (1994: 18) defines a schema as 'a mental representation of a type of object or event that describes only the general characteristics of the type'. They are essentially dynamic, changing and flexible mental structures for organizing our thinking: they adapt, develop and extend as our understanding increases. A more concrete way to explain this is by considering how a schema for 'flower' might be constructed. It might initially be shaped by our life experience of seeing garden flowers such as daffodils and roses, and we might think of flowers as having petals and being coloured. As our knowledge and experience of flowers expands, we might extend our schema to include the understanding that flowers have stalks, buds and seeds, and are fragile. The more we become knowledgeable about flowers, the more the schema can adapt to include variations on the general understanding. So our understanding of a rose as a subset of the flower schema might include knowledge of typical colouring, the fact that it is scented and has thorns, and if we become real experts it might include particular rose varieties, such as 'Peace' or 'Superstar'. A holiday in southern California could expand the schema further by adding a new kind of flower, the desert agave, which only flowers once every 20 years then dies. The general flower schema also adapts and modifies through other linguistic encounters, such as developing an understanding of the metaphorical use of the word 'flower', or specific coinages such as 'flower power'. It might also expand to incorporate compound nouns of the word 'flower', such as 'flowerpot' or 'flowerbed'. One possible representation of this schema for 'flower' is provided in Figure 1.2.

The way that schemata adapt, as described above, to incorporate new understanding is called *accommodation*. Kellogg describes the process of accommodation as having three distinct subprocesses: tuning,

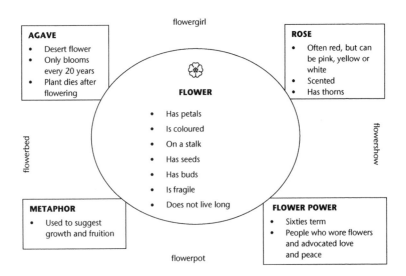

Figure 1.2   A diagram of a schema for 'flower'

accretion, and reorganization. Tuning involves only a minor adjust-ment to the schema, such as paraphrasing a learned concept or defin-ition in your own words. Accretion is a small but more definite change to a schema as a consequence of new information, whereas reorganization is a more fundamental alteration to a schema, perhaps through a sudden new insight (Kellogg 1994: 21).

Schemata then are high-level complex structures used to organize and interpret experience, leading us to predict, expect or understand things on the basis of our existing schemata. In whole class teaching, through talk, the teacher activates a particular knowledge schema for the learners and schematic knowledge therefore 'provides the overall perspective which enables us to integrate what we hear with what we already know, and to fit individual bits of information into a coherent argument' (Cook-Gumperz 1986: 66). So children actively construct knowledge and understanding through interactions between their new knowledge and their previous knowledge; their understanding builds and accumulates upon prior understanding. Schemata of knowledge, stored in the long-term memory, are expanded and modified in the light of new and changing experiences or understandings. Many psychologists (for example, Dochy 1992) have argued that prior knowledge is the strongest determinant of learning. In part this is because prior knowledge is stored in the long-term memory in schemata which 'can easily be retrieved into short term memory. These schemas serve as advance organizers that help to interpret sensory information and link it (organize) to the existing schema and/or schema elements' (Valcke 2002: 152).

Edwards and Mercer (1987) describe this relationship between prior knowledge and new learning as 'the given and the new'; know-ledge is created through 'an interaction between what is already known and what is new' (Edwards and Westgate 1994: 6). Although reading and writing can also support the development of connections between the given and the new, in most educational settings it is talk which has the most potential to support this process. Through talk, children can articulate for themselves what they know and understand, and the process of verbalizing thought in words helps to crystallize emerging understandings.

For talk to be an effective tool for fostering learning, however, there needs to be a level of mutual understanding, 'enough prior shared knowledge to be able to achieve some initial joint understand-ing' (Mercer 2000: 21). Because teachers are frequently very focused upon what they want to teach, it is often easy to ignore or forget what knowledge children have brought into the classroom with them. Wragg and Brown (2001b) describes the teacher who began a lesson on volcanoes, assuming her class knew nothing about them but after giving them an opportunity to tell her what they knew, she discovered that between them they had access to far greater knowledge than she had realized. Children will try to make sense of what they do in the classroom in the light of all their experiences, including those from home or other out-of-school contexts. This can lead to mismatches between teachers' learning focus and children's actual learning, because unanticipated prior knowledge alters what children derive from the learning. Edwards and Mercer (1987) tell of the class undertaking the Island project, designed to investigate social rules and community, but the children thought they were being taught how to survive on a tropical island. Stories and films of survival probably featured more prominently in their prior knowledge than issues of communal living.

Considering knowledge acquired in school from a different perspective, Barnes *et al.* suggest that a lot of what is learned in school is quickly forgotten because no connections are made between school learning and children's own knowledge of the world. School knowledge is not 'integrated into the picture of reality' (Barnes *et al.* 1986: 79) which shapes our actions and understandings. Sometimes this disconnection occurs because the teacher, albeit unwittingly, is keeping too tight a control on the direction of the learning and not giving sufficient opportunity for children to draw on their prior knowledge to make sense of their learning. Kirby analyses the discourse of teacher–pupil interactions whilst reading a storybook together, and found that the talk provided 'limited opportunities for children to connect prior knowledge to the story text' (1996: 14). This contrasts with the teacher referred to earlier in the Hughes and Westgate study who used children's prior knowledge as her starting-point.

Children's potential to learn can be inhibited if 'teachers overestimate learners' abilities to make connections between past and present', and it can be thwarted entirely if what the teacher sees 'as an obvious connection between two experiences may not be apparent to students' (Mercer 2000: 55). Moreover, creating space to establish 'what children already know and understand about a new topic or concept' Wragg (2001: 21) not only supports the development of powerful interconnectivity in learning, but it also reveals to the teacher what the child may have misunderstood. Children's misconceptions are often more informative and more significant foundations for building learning than correct responses. The improvement in the effectiveness of teachers' questioning strategies, reported by Black *et al.* meant that 'teachers learnt more about the pre-knowledge of their pupils, and about any gaps and misconceptions in that knowledge' (2002: 6) and that consequently they were better able to address learners' specific learning needs.

Dialogic talk

One origin of the idea of dialogic talk is the philosophical dialogue conducted by Socrates. Socratic dialogue was a dialectal process in which teacher and student shared a joint inquiry in the search for a truth unknown to both parties. The aim of Socratic dialogue is to promote critical thinking and inquiry, and through a process of consent and dissent to achieve a consensus. It is the process that is important rather than the outcome, because by engaging in genuine dialogue with others, individuals can operate a higher level of thinking than would be possible on their own. Many advocates are keen to distinguish between dialogue, which is a shared movement towards understanding, and discussion, which is adversative and preoccupied by promoting one's own standpoint. Table 1.1, taken from a website describing Socratic dialogue and its uses, illustrates some of the characteristic differences between the two types of talk. From the perspective of whole class teaching, the ways of talking and thinking suggested by the left-hand column represent the kinds of responses that an effective teacher trying to establish a more dialogic interaction might aim to generate.

The notion of the dialogic is also central to the thinking of Bakhtin (1981) who argued that dialogue allowed participants to create new meanings and new understandings, rather than simply reproducing previously constructed understanding. Two key features of dialogic talk are that it builds on participants' prior knowledge, and that it is a process of constructing knowledge together. Wells describes dialogic talk as that in which 'the listener makes sense of what the speaker says by responding to it in terms of his or her own existing knowledge and current purposes' (1999: 289). In comparing the two very different interaction styles of the two teachers in his study, Skidmore (2000) contrasts pedagogical dialogue with dialogic pedagogy. Pedagogical dialogue encompasses the traditional IRF discourse and casts the teacher as the possessor of knowledge which he

Table 1.1 Dialogue and discussion

Partners in dialogue	Discussants
• Investigate a matter • Give each other room to speak • Pose questions in order to understand each other • Reflect back each other's words • Say only what they really mean • Strive for mutual understanding • Have a common understanding of the matter • Make their viewpoint as clear as possible to the other • Are willing to give arguments that support their viewpoints • Investigate differences of opinion • Strive for consensus	• Seek to convince each other that they are right • Demand speaking time • Look upon each other's speaking time as lost time • Undermine each other's standpoints • Attack each other's arguments • Try to make each other's viewpoints seem unintelligible • Strive for approval of their own viewpoint

From http://www.rongen.com/english/socrat/moral.htm

or she must convey to the children. Dialogic pedagogy, on the other hand, is internally persuasive discourse which celebrates 'the primacy of dialogue, the impossibility of any word ever being final' (Skidmore 2000: 284); it has an open structure and fosters interactions which give children plenty of opportunities to think through speaking and listening. In the teaching observed, Skidmore notes 'a chaining of pupil utterances, in which each utterance builds on preceding contributions, qualifying, questioning, or contradicting what previous speakers have said' (2000: 292). In his international study of classroom talk, Alexander found that in addition to the typical patterns of talk identified above, there were some teachers who made greater use of discussion which genuinely attempted to share information and solve problems, and scaffolded dialogue which achieved 'common understanding through structured and cumulative questioning and discussion which guide and prompt, reduce choices, minimise risk and error, and expedite "handover" of concepts and principles' (Alexander 2002: 527). He argues that only discussion and dialogue of this kind can promote talk with sufficient cognitive challenge to support children's learning effectively.

Indeed the most recent and the most comprehensive account of dialogic talk and how it might apply to the classroom is provided by Alexander (2004). He critiques the question–answer–tell routines of conventional teacher discourse and questions whether this kind of teaching deserves to be attributed with the label of 'interactive'. Fundamentally, this kind of talk does not promote real thinking, and frequently offers insufficient cognitive challenge. In contrast, dialogic talk is more searching and deploys interaction strategies, which encourage contributors to work together and to build upon each others' answers. According to Alexander, there are five underlying principles of dialogic talk:

- *collective*: teachers and children address learning tasks together, whether as a group or class;
- *reciprocal*: teachers and children listen to each other, share ideas and consider alternative viewpoints;
- *supportive*: children articulate their ideas freely, without fear of embarrassment over 'wrong' answers; and they help each other to reach common understandings;
- *cumulative*: teachers and children build on their own and each other's ideas and chain them into coherent lines of enquiry;
- *purposeful*: teachers plan and steer classroom talk with specific educational goals in view.

(2004: 27)

The talking and learning classroom

Managing a talk environment which adequately meets the varied learning and behavioural needs of a class of children whilst meeting the requirements of the National Curriculum is a highly complex task, and any account which suggested otherwise would be failing to recognize the high-level teaching skills involved in these kind of interactions. The fact that teachers are more likely to ask factual questions, to dominate the talk time and to direct talk very strongly towards curriculum goals is a reflection of the practical realities of classroom life, not an indictment of teachers' professional competence. Moreover, teachers recognize and value those moments in the classroom when the talking and learning are different in character, when children are questioning, thinking and fired up with enthusiasm, and when the teacher's carefully-formulated plans are set aside in favour of the live flow of 'thinking energy'.

The research described in this chapter is heavily classroom-focused and collectively incorporates a wealth of classroom observations and interviews with teachers. It signals how effective practice can have an impact upon children's participation and learning, and a common theme reverberating through the studies is that altering our speaking and listening practices as teachers is a powerful tool in promoting learning. Mercer (2000) distinguished some of the characteristics of teacher talk which established a lively talking and learning classroom. He found that more effective teachers:

- used question and answer sessions not just to test knowledge, but to guide understanding: 'why' questions to encourage reasoning and reflection;
- used questioning purposefully. All teachers used similar types of question, but the effective teachers chose when and how to use them more skilfully;
- taught not just subject content but procedures for problem-solving and making sense of experience (demonstrating; and explaining the meaning and purpose of class activities etc.);
- treated learning as a social, communicative process; and organized interchange of ideas and mutual support amongst students, encouraged greater participation, relating current activity to past activity.

(summarized from Mercer 2000: 160)

National and international research on teacher talk and classroom interaction provides a rich and reliable insight into relationships between talking, listening and learning. This insight is a potent touchstone by which to consider the quality of interaction and learning in your classroom, and we invite you to share the process of investigating talk in live primary classrooms that the following chapters chronicle, and use this as a stimulus for your own professional development.

2 Investigating teacher talk

A story of involvement

The defining principle of the TALK project was the active and collaborative involvement of teachers throughout all the stages of the research, and as such it stands within the traditions of action research. The traditional model of educational research from the academic perspective positions teachers as the consumer (Leat and Lin 2003): researchers research in order to tell teachers how to teach more effectively. The voices of teachers commenting critically on the findings of research and any subsequent policy built on these findings are rarely heard. Teachers, however, frequently view research as 'ivory towered' and as more theoretical than practical, observing that researchers 'ought to try doing the job'. More recently however, educational policy has actively encouraged the concept of the teacher as researcher, rather than the teacher as the subject of research. The advantage of this approach is seen to be the increased engagement with and ownership of perceived problems and research findings, but also that teachers might look beyond their classrooms for evidence and 'think rigorously about their practice' (OECD 2002: 28) and create a climate in which teachers can become 'critically intelligent' (Prestage *et al.* 2003: 61). Critics of this approach would argue that while engaging in research might enable teachers to reflect on their own practice, it is often less rigorous in its methodological design, weak in evaluating outcomes, and parochial in terms of its application. At its worst, action research has been described as little more than anecdotal accounts of classroom practice (Webb 1996; Foster 1999; Gorard 2002). At its best, it might create a context within which teachers can distinguish between intelligent practice and habitual practice (Ryle 1949). The TALK project sought to exploit the advantage of the university–school collaboration by giving full weight to the teacher as the expert in the classroom, within the context of a methodological framework supported by the research partners from the university, thus allowing the expertise of academic researchers to inform and be informed by professional insight.

The impetus for the TALK project came from the school community, not from the research community; from the start the participating teachers owned the research question and acknowledged it as relevant and pertinent in their own schools. In 1998, following an in-service training day in which schools had met to consider talk and learning in their classrooms, three headteachers approached researchers from Exeter University to ask for support to investigate the nature and quality of teacher talk, given the emphasis on whole class interactive teaching evident within the National Literacy Strategy and National Numeracy Strategy. A subsequent research bid which foregrounded the collaborative nature of the project was successful and was awarded a substantial grant funded by the Economic and Social Research Council (ESRC). Even at this early stage, the headteachers contributed to the application for funding and so were aware from the outset what they were committing themselves to, and so what followed was to a large extent self-inflicted!

The three headteachers were designated key teacher researchers for the project. They were involved at every stage of the research and were the principal bridge between the research community and the school community. Frequent meetings between the heads and the university research team focusing on dialogue and training resulted in the heads being able to collect all the data, then in collaboration with experienced researchers share in the analysis of the results. The original proposal had included a hierarchy of involvement for other teachers within the heads' schools: participant teacher researchers would be involved in discussing the findings and preparing and evaluating teaching materials based on these findings, while participant teachers would allow researchers into their classrooms. This structure was based on an assumption that the extent to which teachers would wish to be involved might vary, and that having roles that allowed for differing levels of involvement might encourage a greater number of teachers to be willing participants. In practice, however, all of the teachers willing to be involved by allowing researchers into their classroom wanted to take an active part in the research and so in the end no distinction was made between teacher researchers and participant teachers. This meant that every teacher who was observed was also part of the process of evaluating the findings, reflecting on the implications, drawing up and piloting guideline materials and participating in the dissemination of the findings.

Launching teachers into research in such a way that avoids the pitfalls outlined by the critics of action research meant attending to those areas of practice and familiarity that belong to the research world rather than the classroom. Two areas in particular stood out: first, rooting the research within the existing research literature, and second, an understanding of the methods of data collection, analysis and interpretation. To address the first issue we ensured that throughout the research period time was set aside for reading, for the headteachers, for the participating teachers and for the researchers. A pattern was set up whereby not everyone read everything, but the reading list was divided up between the teachers and researchers, then through presentation and discussion, the concepts and ideas from the reading were shared within the group. This image of everyone together discussing the ideas and concepts from the perspective of both teachers and researchers perhaps best captures the spirit of the TALK project, a project that was conceived, developed and conducted collaboratively. If this provides an image of the manner in which it was done, then what follows describes how it was done. The 'how' of research is concerned with methodology; this being the second area of expertise that belongs to the research world rather than the classroom. The collaborative approach was also to inform the collecting, analysing and interpreting of the data.

A story of discovery

In describing how we explored classroom talk together, we hope that you will feel encouraged to borrow ideas to investigate and question your own practice. The TALK project did enjoy the luxury of a substantial grant, which paid for a part-time researcher and supply cover to free teachers to participate in the project. Nevertheless the research methods used for the project were varied and on a smaller scale could be tailored and adapted to suit the needs of individual classrooms or schools.

Figure 2.1 shows the overall structure of the research process, but also reveals how the school communities and research community interacted throughout the process. Training days and research days were made possible because of the ESRC funding and played a vital part in drawing on the expertise and contributions from the two

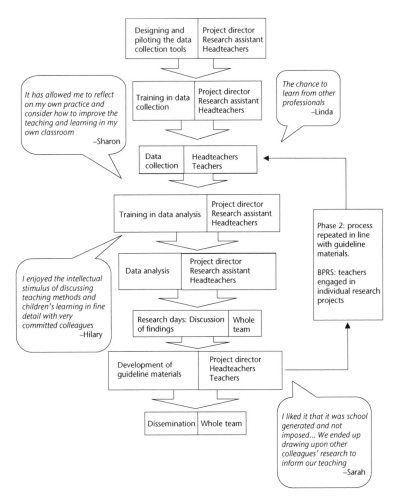

Figure 2.1 The structure and chronology of the TALK project

communities. It is perhaps ironic that a study investigating how teachers use talk to scaffold pupils' learning revealed that creating opportunities for experienced teachers and researchers to talk together scaffolded the professional learning of both groups. The teachers' comments in Figure 2.1 suggest they were perhaps hungry for such an opportunity. For any school or teacher embarking on investigating their own practice, building in time for talk and reflection from the outset might prove profitable.

The TALK project employed four principal research methods, each involving different kinds of data to be collected and analysed. The four methods were:

- analysis of video recordings;
- teacher reflections;
- classroom observations;
- interviewing the children.

Each will be outlined initially in terms of how this data was collected and analysed for the TALK project but with ideas for how these methods might be adapted for more general use to enable you to investigate your own practice.

Investigating classroom talk through the use of video

The idea of allowing a video camera to record 15 to 20-minute episodes of your whole class teaching would probably be alarming to most teachers. That your interactions with the children in your class, captured by these video recordings, would subsequently be watched and analysed by a group of analysts that would include your own headteacher might serve as a considerable disincentive to participate. And finally, that you yourself would be required to watch the recording and reflect on what you saw, may well constitute the final straw with regard to any positive feeling you might have towards being involved with this research project. This, however, was what our participant teachers were willing to do. Each teacher in the project was videoed three times in three different subject areas, making nine times altogether. The different areas were literacy, numeracy and a curriculum area referred to as 'other', being an area for which there was no national strategy. Curriculum areas defined as 'other' included science, art and religious education. Videoing three consecutive lessons within each curriculum area gave a sense of how teacher talk changed as material was first introduced, then subsequently developed over the three lessons. The use of the video camera to capture a complete picture of verbal and physical communication from the teacher, and to a lesser extent from the children, was originally adopted for its efficacy in data collection. Compared to audiotapes or a researcher's observation notes, it was felt that video data would be more comprehensive in what it could capture. Despite a very natural anxiety about teaching in front of the camera, and a clear embarrassment factor at subsequently watching themselves teach, by the end of the project the participant teachers were highly positive about the experience. Ultimately, when writing guideline materials intended to draw on the research findings and offer practical suggestions for improving the use of teacher talk, teachers suggested making more use of a video camera as a strategy to inform and develop classroom practice. Thus a methodological tool for data collection had become a strategy to improve teaching and learning.

Box 2.1 Some practical tips for using a video camera.

- Accommodating the needs of the camera and the needs of the class can be difficult, so allow yourself plenty of playing around time.
- Acclimatize the children to the camera by having it around before you actually use it.
- Decide where the children, you, and the camera will be, to avoid getting in each other's way.
- Decide what will be your focus, you or the children. It is very easy to capture an incomplete record of both.
- Be sure you know what the camera is capturing: we have an amusing collection featuring children's feet, fringes and bottoms!
- Having someone operating the camera only draws attention to it. Once you have sorted out the best position and camera angle, just press record: there is no need for zooming in or panning across the classroom. You are merely keeping a record, not producing art!

The video recordings were used to produce two kinds of data analysis: the teacher reflections outlined below, and the detailed analysis of the teacher talk using a methodology known as the grounded theory approach. This aims to categorize each teacher utterance as having particular features or intentions; these categories emerge from the analysis rather than being predefined. The videos were transcribed so we had a visual and printed record of each lesson. The headteachers attended a training day to develop skills in this approach to analysis. Then together with the project director and research assistant, the task of analysing the video recordings began. The grounded theory approach is both emergent and iterative, and so describing how we got from a video recording and transcript to a fully evolved analysis isn't easy, particularly when five people were involved and their individual analysis needed to be continually cross-validated for inter-coder consistency. Table 2.1 is an attempt to describe what happened.

One of the advantages of this time-consuming and rigorous analysis is that by the end of the process you are very close to the data; you know it very well and can recognize subtle differences between categories. The process of analysing the data gives you a real feel for what is going on in the talk and what are the common characteristics of teacher talk. Again, it was the talk between researchers in arriving at the coding framework that drove the increased understanding of how teachers were using talk in whole class episodes. The results of this analysis appear in following chapters. Of all the research methods used in the TALK project, this highly systematic analysis would perhaps be hardest for you to reproduce in your own classroom. The coding frames, however, now exist. One of the least anticipated but most rewarding outcomes of the TALK project was that 12 of the participant teachers were successfully awarded funding to work for a Best Practice Research Scholarship (BPRS). Some of these teachers used these coding frames to categorize their own teacher talk captured from new video recordings, the hard work of deriving the frameworks having already been done. These coding frames emerged from the analysis of 54 different teaching episodes of 15 to 20 minutes each, but could be used for much smaller scale analysis of videoed lessons. You could very easily take the coding frameworks in Appendix 1, and adapt them to suit the focus of your interest or the time you have available.

 Try it out! Consider videoing yourself working with children in whole class teaching sessions, then analysing your own talk using these coding frames, perhaps focusing on:

- questions only;
- the first five minutes;
- the plenary;
- introducing a new topic;
- recapping.

Table 2.1 The process of coding the video clips

Process	Example
Each researcher independently analysed different lessons, giving each teacher utterance a category which described that interaction. This category was captured on a card system.	A card might look like this, with the code name at the top and examples from the transcript listed below. **Code: Establishing relationships** • Right, well done, I can't see anyone fiddling with pens; that's brilliant. • Well done for getting both of them in. What is clear is that the five researchers might have coded these examples differently, the utterances given in the example could also be seen as examples of 'praise', or 'task management'.
The research team met and shared initial categories, looking tentatively for common categories, or examples of the same categories being coded using a different identifier. No decisions were made at this stage about the categories being used.	In some cases codes might mean the same thing such as 'praise' and 'affirmation' in which case they will be capturing the same data. But terms like 'informing' and 'explaining' are subtly different and so capture different data.
The research team watched and coded one video extract together, discussing decisions and interpretations and beginning to work towards inter-coder consistency.	In one lesson a teacher states that ' "Existing" means it's already there'. Discussions might focus on whether this is an example of 'explaining' and if so how it might differ from 'informing'. Based on these conversations researchers might make new codes or create two codes from one, or even one code from two.

Independent coding continued, in the light of conversations with other coders. As new lessons were coded, new categories emerged and previous categories were refined as appropriate. Each coder had to return to previous coding to check for consistency.	
The research team met to look at all the emerging categories, and to begin the process of definition and cross-validation. It became clear at this stage that some coders focused on the form a statement or question took while others focused on its function.	Coding for form might produce codes such as Factual Question, or Elaborating Statement. Coding for function might produce codes such as Question to Elicit Factual Information, or Question to Develop Content.
Often coders inconsistently coded some utterance for form and others for function. It was decided at this point to code every utterance for both form and function. Four clear forms of question had emerged. Together with five forms of statement	Question: Factual, Speculative, Procedural and Process Statements: Informing, Explaining, Instructing, Socializing and Elaborating
Each researcher continued coding although everyone now had to make sure that every utterance was coded twice: once for form and once for function. Although the coding structure was becoming more fixed, even at this stage new codes were emerging.	The statement: 'You know more than I do' was coded as having the form: Socializing and the function: establishing group relationships.
At a final team meeting the definitive coding frame was decided and everyone made sure their coding was in line with this agreed frame.	See Appendix 1 for final coding frames.

Teacher reflections

Analysing video recordings as we have described above may be an unfamiliar approach, but teachers reflecting on their own practice is much more common. The teachers involved in the TALK project watched their own videos and reflected on what they saw, using a structured set of prompts to stimulate their thinking. This strategy represents a departure from the original research design. In the original design, it was intended that, following the videoed lessons, the headteachers would interview the participating teachers about how they used talk to scaffold pupils' learning. In the end it was decided that using the headteachers as interviewers might be intimidating and inhibit any genuine conversations. The alternative strategy of using post hoc reflections on the video recordings with a prompt schedule proved to be effective in giving the floor to the teachers in a situation that did not place them under any judgement but their own. This valuing of teachers' voices, and belief in their own self-assessment is perhaps why this piece of action research was so enthusiastically received and undertaken by these participating teachers.

Box 2.2   Teachers' voices

- Focusing on a very small aspect of teaching and learning so sharply enabled me to help teachers reflect on their practice for the benefit of pupils' learning. (Leah)
- I have been able to adapt and refine my teaching strategies to stimulate maximum participation from my class. (Mary)
- It has enabled me to consider the participation levels within my own classroom and to reflect upon how different curriculum areas, pairings, resources and the types of talk can influence this participation. (Paula)
- It has enabled me to analyse the impact of different teaching methods I already use and encouraged me to try something new. (Mary)

The prompt sheet designed to support the teachers' reflections began by encouraging the teachers to think about the nature of the class and the purpose of the lessons they had taught before they watched their video. It was important that they recorded this before watching the lesson, so that they made a mental note of what they had intended to do rather than what they believed they had achieved. It is also important that the prompt sheet referred to the words, ideas and concepts of the lesson rather than the curriculum content. This section of the prompt sheet is reproduced in Figure 2.2.

The first hurdle for these teachers, as for most of us, was to get over the embarrassment of watching themselves on video. The second section of the prompt sheet (Figure 2.3) was designed to focus their thinking on the talk they established and on critical moments in that talk, rather than reacting to what they looked like, how they talked, their unknown mannerisms and watching themselves 'being the teacher'. But be reassured, you do get used to seeing yourself on video and these initial reactions do wear off!

The final section of the prompt sheet (Figure 2.4) invited teachers to reflect more generally on how successfully they had used talk to support children's learning in the light of the more focused thinking in section 2.

It was the combined value of watching themselves on video together with the support of focused reflection that teachers found both helpful and informative. Talking with other teachers about the process further enhanced the value of the experience, when it was recognized that as a group they shared similar strengths and weaknesses. Once the findings from the analysis of the video data (as outlined above) were complete, the whole team met for a research day, during which the results from the video analysis were shared. Much of what was revealed by the video analysis might have been construed as negative and disheartening; it was after all their own teaching that was under the spotlight. But the time of sharing findings and discussing implications was highly positive, a mark

---

After the three sessions have been observed, but before you watch the video, answer the following questions:

1. What is this class like to teach in whole class sessions?
2. What did you want the children to learn from these three sessions?
3. On what prior knowledge were you building?
4. What words, ideas or concepts did you introduce?
5. What words, ideas or concepts do you expect them to have learned?

• **Your answers can be either written or taped**

Figure 2.2   Before you start

We'd like you to watch the video and think about the talk in your teaching. We're interested in **your** thoughts and reflections, and there are no right answers. Look for examples of 'critical moments'; times when something interesting or noteworthy related to talk occurs. Some examples are given below – it's unlikely that your video will have examples of all of these. Just pick several 'critical moments' and reflect upon how the talk is operating. We'd like depth rather than breadth – you might well be reflecting on only three to four seconds of talk for each episode.

You will probably find it helpful to watch the video and use the box below to note tape counter numbers or key words describing the episodes of talk you might choose to reflect upon.

Type of talk	Tape counter	Key words
You building on what the children already know.		
You responding to 'wrong' answers.		
You checking the children's understanding.		
You encouraging children to develop their thinking.		
You clarifying children's misunderstanding.		
You explaining a new idea/concept/word.		
A time when the talk went well.		
A time when the talk went less well.		
A time when you didn't pursue whether a child misunderstood.		
Other		

• **Write or tape your reflections on these critical moments**

Figure 2.3   It's good to talk

Having reflected upon your 'critical moments', please consider the following questions, and write or record your responses.

1. What have you learned about how you use talk as a teacher?
2. Do you think the children learned the words, concepts or ideas that you wanted them to learn?
3. What are your strengths in whole class teaching?
4. What would you like to build on or develop?

Figure 2.4   Final thoughts

of these teachers' commitment to learning, both for themselves as professionals and for the children in their classes. Being fully involved in the process of capturing classroom talk, analysing and reflecting on it seemed to create a sense of ownership of the research; they weren't being told by an outside 'expert' what was effective and ineffective, they had been part of the process of discovery. And, of course, what they were discovering was echoed in the research literature they were reading; the issues being raised were shared by a wider community of teachers than themselves. Moreover, explicitly drawing out common threads and concerns initiated some perceptive critiquing of national strategies which have increased the emphasis on whole class teaching, but have also stressed the importance of pace and of meeting curriculum goals.

> **Try it out!** The approach we used is readily adaptable for use in your school. As a teaching staff, or a curriculum subject team, you could each video a 15-minute episode of your teaching, and then reflect on it, using a prompt sheet as above. It might be an idea to adapt or devise a different prompt sheet collectively as a team as part of the process of investigation. After each teacher has had time to watch their video and complete the reflection, arrange a time for group discussion and sharing of findings, and complete the process by determining what action to take as a consequence.

Classroom observation

You will already be well aware from your own classrooms that not all children engage with equal enthusiasm in whole class teaching episodes. For a teacher working with up to 30 children, following the individual participation of any one child is impossible, particularly if children are quietly disengaging. The TALK project used a structured observation grid (Table 2.2) to observe four children in all 54 lessons being videoed. The four children were a high-achieving boy and girl and a low-achieving boy and girl, a selection that allowed us to compare participation and interaction levels for gender and achievement. Using structured observation can be informative for any teacher wishing to track the participation of individual children or groups of children in their class. Clearly this grid requires an independent observer to be sitting in on the lesson with no other responsibility other than completing the schedule by tallying in the appropriate boxes when a given behaviour occurs. What systematic observation offers is a picture of how engaged or disengaged selected children are, and how successfully teachers hold the attention of, for example, less able children. Observing off-task behaviours every five minutes

Table 2.2 The classroom observation grid

	HA Girl				HA Boy				LA Girl				LA Boy			
Puts hand up																
Answers question after invitation																
Joins in collective response																
Asks question																
CHILD INITIATES TALK WITH TEACHER																
Task related																
Task unrelated																
SHOUTS OUT																
Task related																
Task unrelated																
OFF-TASK BEHAVIOURS Record every 5 minutes	5	10	15	20	5	10	15	20	5	10	15	20	5	10	15	20
Fiddling and fidgeting																
Not looking to the front																
Talking to neighbour																
Off-Task Rate 1–4																

reveals at what point in the session children become disengaged. If there is a general tendency for low-ability children to be less engaged after 10 to 15 minutes, for example, then this argues strongly for keeping the whole class sessions shorter, or including more variety in the opportunities to participate. If observing children in different curriculum areas reveals that they are generally more engaged in numeracy, for example, you might reflect on what you do in numeracy which increases their engagement.

A common observation of groups of children interacting with a single teacher is that certain children stand out as being more vocal, more frequently given the floor or more generally noticeable than others. An observation grid such as this would not be needed to identify children who are disruptive or who shout out. What this kind of grid can reveal however is how inclusive these sessions are. There will be children who will dominate any question and answer time and others who rarely contribute. Two revealing aspects of the observation grid (Table 2.2) are the noting of questions asked by children, rather than by the teacher, and the number of times the teacher invites a child to answer a question. The nature of these whole class episodes is such that a child's opportunity to contribute is almost entirely governed by whether the teacher selects him or her to speak or not. In a class of 30 children, and a time period of less than 20 minutes, no one child will be given many opportunities to speak; a pertinent question might be how many children never speak at all. Systematically observing children who seem to be reluctant participants might be revealing. Care has to be taken however: a child who sits quietly and rarely volunteers information might still be highly engaged, while a child with a hand permanently in the air might be doing so habitually rather than because they have anything to say. Nevertheless, taken together the behaviours that imply engagement and those that imply disengagement can be informative. What was revealed from these classroom observations from the TALK project data, and a discussion of what these findings imply for teaching that increases levels of interactivity can be found in Chapter 3. This data comes from 54 observations and so can reveal average data for how often children in general participate, or how often they disengage. Such a large-scale data set also allowed for gender and achievement groups to be compared. For individual teachers, however, there might be the opportunity to track certain children and get a picture of what kinds of teacher talk will increase or decrease their levels of engagement. Explicit observation of this kind can provide the third eye that you can never have yourself when you are involved with directing the questioning and talk to facilitate the learning of up to 30 children.

Try it out! Use this grid, or an adapted version of it, to investigate participation levels in several classes, or in different curriculum subjects in your school. You could use it to track a particular group of children that you are concerned about such as your gifted and talented children, the traveller children, children with English as an additional language, or underachieving boys. Avoid having more than four children as your focus as it is too difficult to observe more than four. It might be possible to train classroom assistants, some willing parents, or some governors to conduct the observations for you.

Interviewing the children

The four focus children who were observed in each of the videoed lessons were also interviewed by the headteachers following each completed cycle of three lessons. Thus each group of four children were interviewed three times, once for each subject area. The interview was designed to explore what the children had remembered and understood from the lesson and also what they had misunderstood. It was also the intention of the interview to ascertain what the children believed the main point of the lesson was. Questions were also provided by the teacher who had taught the lessons. These reflected the teacher's beliefs and expectations concerning the relative importance of what was covered in the lessons. The interview began and ended with the same question (see Figure 2.5), on the assumption that the process of talking through the lesson might clarify for the child what the lesson had been about.

It can be a salutary experience to discover what children believe your carefully planned lesson, complete with clearly defined aims and objectives, was actually about! From the perspective of the research project, the purpose of the children's interview was to check what the children had taken away from the lesson. From a teaching and learning perspective, however, an interview such as this makes visible any discrepancy between what the teacher believes they have taught

- What do you think was the most important thing you have learned in the three literacy lessons?
- Did you know anything about this already? Tell me what you knew?
- Did you find anything hard to understand?
- If you had to explain this to your mum and dad, how would you explain it? Pretend you're the teacher!

Teachers' questions
(*Questions supplied by the teacher relating to the details of the lesson, and reflecting what the teacher had hoped they would learn and see as important*)

Final question (repeat of first question)
- What do you think was the most important thing you have learned in the three literacy lessons?

Figure 2.5 Child interview questions

and what the child reveals they have learnt. In an interview the child has the floor; if talking through ideas does provide an opportunity to make and construct meaning, then the interview process may support learning. In another research project, conducted by the same university research team, secondary-aged children were interviewed following writing tasks. The interviews attempted to help the children articulate the choices and decisions they were making as they wrote: what prompted them to cross out and alter writing; when they stop and think, what are they planning, the next word, the form of the sentence, the shape of the paragraph? The children were interviewed three times, but one of these interviews fell at a point where a piece of work was half finished. Several of the children commented on the research process itself, affirming that the process of reflecting on their thinking, on making explicit what they were doing and why they were doing it, helped them when they subsequently continued the piece of writing. In a similar way, it is perhaps unsurprising that when we repeated the opening question at the end of the TALK project interview, the quality of children's responses to the same question had often improved.

There are ways you could adapt what we did and use 'interviewing' in your own classroom both to strengthen your understanding of individual children's grasp of the learning in hand, and to give them opportunities to articulate their own learning:

- using plenary time to interview individuals while the rest of the class do a different plenary task;
- asking children to interview each other about their learning and report back;
- inviting children to devise appropriate interview questions for each other based on the topic being learned;
- using classroom assistants, or other adults, to conduct interviews and report back to you.

Conclusion

The TALK project was a process of action research in which teachers and researchers collaborated to explore and discover how teacher talk could be best used to support learning. One of the interesting aspects of developing the research was the discovery that tools developed for data collection have the potential to become tools to support children's learning, in the case of the children's interviews, and to support the teacher's reflective practice in the case of the teacher reflections.

The outcomes and classroom implications of this research in terms of the findings that resulted from the investigations into classroom talk outlined in this chapter are described in more detail in the following chapters. If you wish to try out any of the ideas in this chapter to explore talk in your own classroom or school, it is well worth looking in more detail at the following chapters as they will give you ideas on how you might adapt the video analysis, observation grids, the reflective prompt sheet or interview questions to suit your needs and interests.

There were, however, other outcomes not recorded in this book. Twelve teachers felt enthusiastic and confident enough to engage in personal research projects based on the implications of the TALK project, through working for Best Practice Research Scholarships, and the results of their research made their way into their own school's development plans. The quality of the professional learning for the teachers involved was perhaps one of the most significant outcomes of the TALK project. The headteachers presented the research at the British Educational Research Conference in 2002 and at the European Association for Research in Learning and Instruction in Padua in 2003. At both conferences, practising teachers are few and far between. The success of the TALK project confirms the value of collaborative research between schools and universities, and demonstrates that high quality, academically rigorous research is not incompatible with teacher research.

3 Interactive teaching

Interactive teaching – a national policy initiative

Perhaps the archetypal picture of teaching is that of the teacher standing at the front of the class engaged in dialogue with children. Implicit in this image is the notion of interaction, though at different times in educational history and in different contexts the nature of that interaction changes. At one extreme, some classrooms are typified by an interaction pattern where teachers are the speakers and children are the listeners; at the other extreme are classrooms where the teacher and the children interact through discussion and dialogue involving both speaking and listening. In recent years, the policy initiatives of the National Literacy Strategy (DfEE 1998) and the National Numeracy Strategy (DfEE 1999) have redirected pedagogic attention to classroom interaction, and have invested heavily in interactive whole class teaching as the heart of these strategies. In both strategies, high-quality whole class teaching is promoted as the pathway to raising standards, and both strategies emphasize the importance of pacy, participatory and challenging interaction in achieving effective whole class teaching. Table 3.1 illustrates this by extracting some of the references to interactive teaching from the two strategy frameworks.

The training materials and videos for both the National Literacy and Numeracy Strategies have also emphasized interactive whole class teaching and have provided models of good practice and examples of teaching strategies which will support vibrant interaction. The current significance of interactive teaching in the national educational context is further underlined by its explicit inclusion in the Standards for the Award of Qualified Teacher Status (DfES 2002): all trainee teachers will need to demonstrate their ability to 'employ interactive teaching methods' in order to be awarded QTS.

Table 3.1 Frameworks for teaching

NLS: Framework for teaching	NNS: Framework for teaching
Successful literacy instruction occurs when teaching is: • discursive – characterized by high quality oral work • interactive – pupils' contributions are encouraged, expected, and extended (p.8)	Successful numeracy instruction occurs when teachers: • structure their mathematics lessons and maintain a good pace; • devote a high proportion of lesson time to direct teaching of whole classes and groups; • question pupils effectively, including as many of them as possible, giving them time to think before answering, targeting individuals to take account of their attainment and needs, asking them to demonstrate and explain their methods and reasoning, and exploring reasons for any wrong answers.
Whole class teaching is most effective when 'it is interactive, delivered at a good pace' (p.112)	Effective numeracy teaching involves 'direct teaching and inter-active oral work with the whole class and groups';
'Careful management of demands and responses in whole-class and group sessions offer high levels of involvement for all pupils, particularly the least able, many of whom quickly gain in confidence' (p.10)	'High-quality direct teaching is oral, interactive and lively. It is not achieved by adopting a simplistic formula of "drill and practice" and lecturing the class, or by expecting pupils to teach themselves from books. It is a two-way process in which pupils are expected to play an active part by answering questions, contributing points to discussions, and explaining and demonstrating their methods to the class.' (NNS Direct teaching)

Why the emphasis on interactive teaching?

The policy move to strong advocacy of whole class interactive teaching was prompted principally by the school effectiveness research of Reynolds and Farrell (1996) who argued that high standards and interactive teaching were associated. Drawing on international perspectives, they found that pedagogic practice in countries such as Korea and Japan, who performed strongly in international comparisons of children's academic attainment, was heavily oriented towards interactive whole class teaching. This teaching included all children, regardless of ability level, and set high expectations of what children could achieve. Reynolds and Farrell's research, however, takes little account of the differing cultural contexts in which the teachers were operating: in particular, the differences in motivation and educational aspiration of Pacific Rim countries when compared with the UK, and the differential impact of societal structures, such as class, on attainment in different countries. Moreover, others including Alexander (2004) have criticized the basis of the research as flawed because of the simplistic correlations it draws between high attainment and whole class teaching, when similar claims could be made for the relationship between low attainment and whole class teaching, in Africa, for example. As Alexander notes 'direct instruction through whole class teaching is the commonest teaching approach world-wide so it is as strongly associated with low educational standards as with high' (2004: 17).

No doubt policymakers were also influenced by parallel concerns that the emphasis on topic work, conducted principally in groups, was responsible for perceived lower standards in England. Several research studies, such as that by Bennett *et al.* (1984), had critiqued the effectiveness of group work and the claims made for the benefits of peer interaction in groups. Instead, they argued, group work was more of an organizational strategy with children arranged in groups but nonetheless tending to work as individuals within that group. Major changes to primary teaching were thus made without any systematic consultation with primary teachers and were fuelled by a deficit model of primary teaching more concerned with what teachers and children did not do well, rather than with any successful practice or attainment. This, when combined with a punitive Ofsted inspection regime, as Corden points out, was 'hardly designed to encourage professional conscientiousness and commitment' (2000: 47). In contrast, the underlying philosophy of the TALK project was to involve teachers in the process of examining their own classroom interaction, and working together collaboratively to improve it.

The relationship between effective interaction and learning

The centrality of talk and effective interaction in creating classrooms where children can learn should not be underestimated, as has been explored in Chapter 1. Talk is the dominant medium for teaching and learning; both teachers and learners use talk to support learning more during a school day than they use either reading or writing. It is something of an irony therefore that in the UK assessment is predominantly undertaken through the written mode, unlike many European countries which make far greater use of assessing learning through the spoken mode. How teachers use talk in whole class interaction and how they create opportunities for lively peer to peer interaction should be central considerations in both planning and teaching.

Contemporary psychological theories of learning such as those proposed by Bruner (1986) and Vygotsky (1986) emphasize the way the child constructs meaning through interactions – with other people, with different contexts, and with different experiences. The learner's understanding 'is constantly interacting with the perceived real world and adjusting itself to it' (Barnes *et al.* 1986). So children's knowledge and understanding are expanded and modified in the light of new and changing experiences or understandings. In the process of developing learning through talk, 'children are active constructors of their own knowledge' (Wells 1986: 65) rather than passive recipients of the teacher's wisdom. The image of Dickens' Mr Gradgrind with his obsessive preoccupation with facts, and the hitherto common metaphor of 'drumming things in to children's heads' both reflect dated understandings about how children learn. But Wells highlights that to enable this active construction of knowledge children need 'evidence, guidance and support'. In purposeful whole class teaching, then, children and teachers are co-constructors of knowledge. So for the teacher, a primary responsibility is to enable the connections to be made between the 'already known' and the 'new', to lead children from their present understanding to new understandings within their zone of proximal development

(Vygotsky 1986) – that developmental area where the child can achieve something with support which he or she should eventually be able to achieve independently.

Thus the teacher is not a passive facilitator but an expert guide, who offers both challenge and support to learners and assists in the process of constructing new meanings and knowledge. The idea of 'guided participation', promoted by Barbara Rogoff (1991) and discussed earlier in Chapter 1, is pertinent here. In the National Literacy Strategy, the practices of guided reading and guided writing draw on this idea. Rogoff's argument that 'interaction with other people assists children in their development by guiding their participation in relevant activities' (1991: 191) underpins the theoretical principles of guided reading and writing, and it is through talk that this supportive guiding is enabled to occur. In essence, contemporary thinking about learning asserts the inefficacy of transmission models of teaching, rejecting the possibility that the knowledge of the teacher can be transmitted directly to the learner. Instead effective interaction with the expert guide helps children to engage, to understand and to remember.

One example in the TALK project of a teacher acting as an expert guide occurred in a Year 2 numeracy lesson, where the teacher used careful managed questioning to probe Susie's understanding of the pattern evident in the five times table. When Susie's first response is unclear, the teacher presses her again for a clearer answer, rather than moving on to another child who will give the right answer. Then, when Susie's second response moves towards the right answer, she challenges the rest of the class to think about Susie's answer and furnish the missing details.

Teacher: Would anyone like to explain to me how they know their number is in the 5 times table? . . .

Susie: If it's in the five times table it means it's like, the number.

Teacher: Come on, Susie, we were just doing it together just then.

Susie: If it's in the fives times table it always has a five in it.

Teacher: [The teacher turns back to address the whole class.] Right, Susie was almost there, when she said it's *always* got a five on the end. She's not quite there is she? Who can add just that little bit that she needs to make it quite right? Ryan? Sean? Ok, don't worry. Olivia? [Olivia has put her hand up.]

Olivia: It's either got 5 or a 0.

Teacher: Or a 0. Well done, do you remember now . . . it ends in a 5 or a 0, so if yours ended with a 5 or a 0 [glances around room] then you're bound to be right. Well done. Very good. OK.

Whole class interactive teaching: a definition

Despite the fact that 'interactive teaching' is now a commonplace term, it is nonetheless a term used with remarkably little shared understanding. After all, it seems axiomatic, as Williams *et al.* (1998) claim, that all teaching is interactive in that it involves communication between a teacher and learners. Yet only a brief discussion amongst teachers reveals that there are multiple ways of interpreting the word 'interactive'.

Box 3.1 Talking point
• What is your 'instant definition' of interactive teaching?   • Is there any teaching which is not interactive?   • What kinds of teaching are more interactive or less interactive?

Varying interpretations of interactivity abound in educational literature. Following the Bullock Report and its emphasis on the importance of talk, Barnes (1976: 114–15) drew a distinction between transmission teaching and interpretation teaching. He based his distinction between the two on a notion of equality or balance in the exchanges between teachers and children, and he talked about *asymmetric* discourse, where the balance of control and quantity of talk was in the teacher's favour, and *interactive* discourse where there was a more equal balance in contributions made by both teachers and pupils. Clearly, in terms of whole class teaching, this kind of balance is much harder to achieve because of the ratio of one teacher to about 30 pupils; this was, in part, why Barnes and the Bullock Report were so keen to foster better use of group talk. The National Literacy Strategy is explicit that is 'not a recipe for transmission teaching' (DfEE 1998: 8), but neither of the national strategies grapple with the difficulty in achieving interactive teaching in a whole class context where there is one teacher and a large number of children.

A somewhat different view of interactivity is proposed by Cooper and McIntyre (1994). They suggest that classroom interaction can be thought of in terms of a continuum through four stages: from transmissive, where teachers cover curriculum content through direct instructional strategies, through to interactive teaching, then reactive teaching, and finally to self-directed learning, where the student is managing his or her learning independently. In effect, however, Cooper and MacIntyre focus upon the interactive–reactive element of the continuum as being the predominant range of interaction patterns evident in most teaching scenarios. They define interactive teaching as those interactions where teachers integrate into their plans their knowledge of pupils, but 'the teacher sees the proper use of pupil input as being only within the parameters set by his pre-active lesson plans' (Cooper and MacIntyre 1994: 639). Reactive teaching, by contrast, is characterized by the teacher's willingness to adjust learning objectives to accommodate the interests of the pupils.

Cooper and McIntyre's definition of interactive teaching clearly does not see it as the optimum mode; instead it is strongly teacher-led on the teacher's terms, and is less likely to promote a pathway to independent learning. Their interpretation is probably closest to that offered in the National Literacy and Numeracy Strategies training materials. Mroz *et al.* (2000) note that the impression from training models promoted by the national strategies implies that interaction comprises quick-fire question and answer work within highly teacher-controlled dialogue. However by signalling the importance of reactive interactions, Cooper and McIntyre are more closely aligned to the ideas of Bruner and Vygotsky and guiding learners with support to a point of independence.

More recently, Hargreaves *et al.* (2002) for example define interactivity as the relationship between the number of statements and questions: 'interactivity depends on the ratio of questions to statements' – the higher the ratio of questions to statements, the more interactive the teaching. Despite its surface clarity, this definition is problematic for several reasons. It appears to take as its paramount principle that interactivity is about the number of opportunities pupils are given to make a contribution, without any corresponding emphasis given either to the quality of that contribution or the level of participation of a wide range of pupils. So a quick-fire question and answer episode in which four or five children gave several answers would be deemed interactive, even though the majority of children in the class had made no contribution at all. Second, by pinning a measure of interactivity on the number of questions asked, the authors make interactivity very much about supplying answers to teachers' questions. Yet other research has shown that a high number of questions on the teacher's part tends to reduce the quantity and quality of children's responses. Wood (1988: 143) found that a high frequency of questions in teacher's talk tended to 'generate relatively silent children and to inhibit any discussion between them'. The more questions teachers ask, the less children say. The example below from a Year 2 science lesson is a pacy sequence of questioning, which would be classified as interactive under English *et al.*'s terms, but many teachers would contest whether this is genuinely interactive:

> *Teacher:*   What they are going to need? A jar?
> *Children:* Yes.
> *Teacher:*   A paper towel?
> *Children:* Yes.
> *Teacher:*   Water?
> *Children:* Yes.
> *Teacher:*   A label?
> *Children:* Yes.
> *Teacher:*   A pencil to write the label with?
> *Children:* Yes.
> *Teacher:*   Is that it?
> *Children:* Broad beans.
> *Teacher:*   You'll need a broad bean as well, won't you?

In all the above interpretations of interactive teaching, there is an assumption that in some way it must involve children's spoken responses. Implicitly, therefore, they all assume that listening is a passive activity. Yet listening to a story, for example, could be argued to be a highly interactive experience in which the listener has to interpret the speaker's words, visualize characters and events, anticipate the plot, and empathize with characters and their situations. At its best, listening to a story is an act of imaginative engagement. Equally, in terms of modern technology, the term 'interactive' is used frequently, not to describe spoken interactions, but to describe the user's ability to control, change or respond to a medium (interactive TV, for example).

Too much teacher talk?

Managing interactions with a class of up to 30 pupils in a whole class context is a highly complex undertaking. Research has frequently indicated that teachers tend to dominate whole class talk – what Barnes called 'asymmetric discourse'. This awareness was one of the principal reasons that group and pair work were so strongly advocated as effective strategies in the post-Bullock era. One impact of a renewed emphasis upon whole class teaching may be to return to a situation where teachers talk a lot and children listen (or don't listen!) a lot. Indeed, the research of Hargreaves *et al.* (2002), already referred to in Chapter 1, has indicated how brief the spoken contributions by children tend to be. Arguably, this pattern is endorsed by the National Literacy and Numeracy Strategies as many of the training videos show high levels of teacher talk relative to children's talk. For example, the *Grammar for Writing* video features a sequence where the teacher leads a shared writing session on creating suspense in narrative. On one level, the sequence shows high expectations of children's understanding of language features, and considerable enthusiasm and energy on the part of the teacher. On a different level, the sequence is characterized by lengthy teacher contributions and very short responses from the children. The text below from a Year 6 literacy lesson by presenting the spoken words in an unreadable font highlights graphically how the pattern of teacher–child talk can be heavily dominated by the teacher.

Child: τ σαιδ τηατ πεοπλε ωιλλ σπενδ τηειρ μονεψ ον γαμε μαχηινεσ τξ

Teacher: Σο ενχουραγινγ χηιλδρεν το γαμβλε ανδ το σπενδ μονεψ, ψεσ? Ωηατ αρε σομε οφ τηε ισσυεσ? Ωε ωεσαιδ αβουτ τηε τραφφιχ τηινγ, υο βρουγητ τηατ υπ εαρλιερ ανδ ωε σαιδ τηερε σ γοινγ το βε αν ινχρεασε ιν τραφφιχ. Ωηατ αρε τηε τωο σορτ οφ προβλεμσ αβουτ τηισ ινχρεασε ιν τραφφιχ? Ιτ σ γοιν γ το λεαδ το τωο τηινγσ, τηερε αρε τωο σορτ οφ ισσυεσ ωιτη τηερε βεινγ μορε τραφφιχ, κνοχκ–ον εφφε χτσ οφ τηερε βεινγ μορε τραφφιχ. Οωεν?

Child: τ?λλ?πολλυτε?τηε?αιρ? ?τξ??

Teacher: Πολλυτιον, ανδ τηε οτηερ ονε ισ? Ωηατ? Ατ τηε τοπ τηερε?

Child: οισε.

Teacher: Ωελλ, ψεσ, νοισε χαν βε πολλυτιον. Ωε κνοω νοισε πολλυτιον.

Child: Παρκινγ

Teacher: Ριγητ, παρκινγ, τηατ σ ανοτηερ ισσυε. Σο φορ τραφφιχ ωε ρε γοινγ το ηαωε παρκινγ προβλεμσ ανδ πολλυτιον προβλεμσ. Οκ, νοω, ψου αρε, ωηεν ψου ωριτε αν αργυμεντ, φυστ λικε ψου σαω λαστ ωεεκ ωιτη Μρσ Ωελση ωηεν σηε ταυγητ ψου, λοοκινγ ατ διφφερεντ ωαψσ το συππορτ ψουρ αργυμεντ. Βεχα υσε ωηατ σ τηε πυρποσε ωηεν ψου ωριτε ορ ψου σαψ αν αργυμεντ? Ωηατ αρε ψου τρψινγ το δο? Ωη ατ ισ τηε πυρποσε οφ ψουρ ωριτινγ? Ωηατ αμ Ι τρψινγ το δο ηερε? Ι κνοω Ι ωροτε τηισ το τρψ ανδ ση οω ψου α ποιντ βυτ φυστ πρετενδ Ι διδν τ, φυστ πρετενδ Ι ωροτε τηισ βεχαυσε τηισ ισ ωηατ Ι βελιεωε. Ωηατ αμ Ι τρψινγ το δο ωιτη τηισ πιεχε οφ ωριτινγ? υαμιε?

Child: ακε?τηε?χουνχιλ?νοτ?βυιλδ?τηε?λεισυρε?χεντρε?

Teacher: Ριγητ, Ι μ τρψινγ το μακε σομεβοδψ αγρεε ωιτη μψ ποιντ οφ ωιεω, αρεν τΙ? Ι μ τρψινγ το περσυαδε τηεμ, αλριγητ, ανδ τηερε αρε διφφερεντ ωαψσ ιν ωηιχη ψου χαν χηανγε ψουρ ωριτινγ ορ τηινγσ τηατ ψου χαν αδδ το ψουρ ωριτινγ το μακε ψουρ ωριτινγ σεεμ μορε περσυασιωε, οκ? Νοω, ονε ωαψ ιν ωηι χη ψου χαν δο τηισ ισ – ψου διδ δο τηισ ωιτη Μρσ Ωελση διδν τ ψου? Διδ ψου λοοκ ατ σομε γραπησ ανδ τηινγσ?

Children: οο

Teacher: Ριγητ, ονε ωαψ ιν ωηιχη ψου χαν δο τηισ ισ το πυτ στατιστιχσ ιντο ψουρ αργυμεντ σο ψου χαν σαψ Ι μ ριγητ βεχαυσε σομεβοδψ ηασ δονε α συρωεψ ανδ τηεψ ηαωε αχτυαλλψ φουνδ τηισ ουτ. Ι μ νοτ φυστ μακινγ τηισ υπ, τηισ ισ ρεαλ βεχαυσε σομεβοδψ ηασ αχτυαλλψ γονε ανδ τηεψ αρε βαχκινγ υπ ωηατ Ι αμ σαψινγ. Χαν ψου σεε ιν τηατ πιεχε οφ ωριτινγ ωηερε Ι ηαωε υσεδ στατιστιχσ το βαχκ υπ μ ψ αργυμεντ? Χαν ψου φινδ αν εξαμπλε, ψου ρε λοοκινγ φορ νυμβερσ, τηατ σ α βιγ χλυε, λοοκινγ φορ νυμβερσ. Πετε?

However this pattern is not the only pattern. The balance between teacher contributions and child contributions can be very different as in the extract below from another Year 6 literacy lesson. By drawing on the children's own experiences, many of the children's responses in this discussion were more than 20 words long, and Joe's response is 69 words. Moreover, the teacher encourages Thomas to extend and elaborate upon his original contribution by her use of questioning.

Teacher: So can you think of . . . if you were either really naughty or a really funny time, or a time you were really scared [children put their hands up]. Thomas?

Thomas: I took a long piece of wood off a branch and hit on to my brother's head.

Teacher: Why did you do it?

Thomas: I don't know.

Teacher: Did you do it to hurt him, had he made you cross?

Thomas: No, he kept bugging me so he was walking along the garden and I lobbed it and it just bounced off the top of his head.

. . .

Joe: Um, me and Jamie was making a swing at the end of the close, and then I got up in the tree and he got up in the tree and I started jumping on the branch, and he was sitting on it and he swinged round and I stamped on the branch really hard and the branch snapped and I went with the branch and landed on Jamie's head [children laugh].

Interaction and participation

Effective whole class interaction, however, is not simply about the nature of exchanges or the patterns of talk between teachers and children. It is also about involvement and participation. The key distinction between interaction in a whole class context and other contexts for interaction, such as groups or one to one, is that the teacher has to manage the interaction with about 30 pupils. In most social situations involving groups of this size, there are a considerable number of individuals who are reluctant to volunteer to speak, and those who are very keen to do so, and primary classrooms are no different. The teachers in the TALK project articulated very strong beliefs that good whole class teaching would be marked by high levels of participation and even before watching the video recordings of their own teaching, they were aware of the difficulties in achieving high levels of involvement in whole class talk.

Both the National Strategies for Literacy and Numeracy emphasize the importance of involvement in whole class teaching, and assert that whole class teaching is an appropriate setting for differentiation. The NNS notes that one of the factors that promotes high standards in mathematics is the ability to 'involve pupils and

---

Box 3.2 Teachers' voices

- 'It is a large class of 34 . . . I am aware that there are a few who do not contribute unless they are prompted and many would dominate the entire lesson with their responses. Using white-boards helps to combat this but there is not much space for one each and there are still some who do not give much. They respond best to pacy lessons where a variety of teaching methods and visual aids are used.'
- 'I am continuously aware of the "fringe" children – the children who sit around the edges and appear to be listening and doing the right things but actually have little or no input unless questioned.'
- 'It is quite challenging to teach the class in whole class sessions because of the spectrum of ability . . . there are some behaviour issues with children who find it hard to maintain concentration. I worry that when focusing on keeping some children's attention, I may be losing others and more able attention.'
- 'The proportion of children who contribute in these sessions has risen over the year, although some despite being focused and attentive still do not volunteer information readily.'

---

maintain their interest through appropriately demanding work' (DfEE 1999a: 5). Likewise, the National Literacy Strategy suggests that whole class teaching in literacy is an effective mechanism for generating high levels of involvement: 'By using common texts and activities, the teacher can hold the class together yet maximise participation and challenge children at different levels' (DfEE 1998: 100). However the research of Hargreaves *et al.* (2002) indicated that whilst teaching was indeed pacy and characterized by high levels of teacher questioning, the average length of any talk contribution made by a child was just four words – hardly a high level of involvement! In the TALK project, we looked at participation and involvement from a further perspective – which children participated in interactions with the teacher. The classroom observations of four focus children of differing gender and ability (high-ability boy and girl; low-ability boy and girl) revealed participation patterns that suggest that some groups of children may be more likely to become involved in whole class teaching than others.

In terms of the levels of response to whole class teaching according to the child's ability, there are clear differences between the groups. High-achieving children adopted a considerably more positive participation role than their lower-achieving peers. They were markedly more likely to volunteer a response through putting their hands up and they were more likely to join in a collective class response, such as reading a sentence aloud together. Conversely, they were less likely to be off-task during whole class teaching. One mark of the teachers' commitment to equal participation is that high-achieving children were only marginally more likely to be selected to give an answer. However, this does not redress the imbalance in the participation rates according to ability as it only equalizes between those who have put their hand up. The lower achievers who did not volunteer are self-excluded from this strategy.

Curiously, a very similar pattern emerged for participation according to the gender of the child. Girls, like high achievers, were more positively participatory; they were more likely to offer to respond through putting a hand up, they were more likely to join in a

Table 3.2   Pattern of interaction by gender

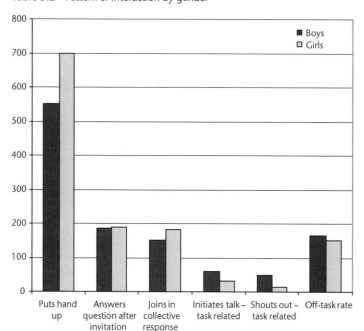

collective response and less likely to be off-task. It is noticeable, though, that boys were more likely to initiate task-related talk or shout out something relevant to the task. These are behaviours which may well run counter to the behaviour management of whole class teaching, but they do signal that boys may not be completely disinterested; however, they may well be less willing to play by the conventional classroom rules of putting up a hand and waiting to be invited to answer. Girls may be much more comfortable operating within the boundaries of these classroom conventions.

These patterns of participation, varying as they do according to the ability and the gender of the child, suggest that 'interactivity' is experienced differently for different children, and that whole class teaching may not be as inclusive as the national strategies advocate. Significantly, this may mean that some children benefit more from whole class teaching than others; in this case, high achievers and girls appear to be participating in learning more actively than low

Table 3.3 Patterns of interaction by achievement levels

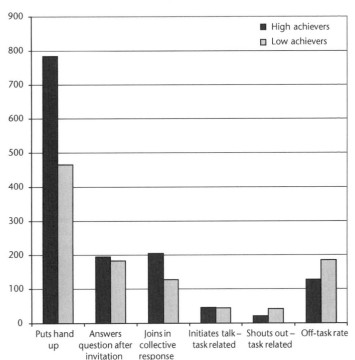

achievers and boys. Given the national and international concern about underachieving boys, these patterns of participation suggest that whole class teaching could be exacerbating the problem of boys' underachievement.

The opportunity to step back from the routines of classroom teaching and to reflect upon the video sequences of their own teaching enabled the teachers in the TALK project to determine for themselves what they perceived as areas for development in their own classrooms. The commitment to encouraging the highest possible levels of participation in whole class teaching was strengthened when the teachers recognized in the video capture of their own teaching that participation remained patchy.

Box 3.3 Teachers' voices

- 'Only a few children responded by putting their hands up.'
- 'I need to ensure as an outcome that all children are involved.'
- 'I would like to have more impact on the whole class.'
- 'Talk in the classroom is very much directed towards those children who have the confidence to put their hand up.'
- 'I would like even more involvement.'
- 'I need to make a conscious effort to scan around the group more so that these things [non-participation] don't go unnoticed.'

Generating involvement in interactive teaching

Whilst there may be questions about the extent to which whole class teaching is genuinely interactive, there are also plenty of possibilities for making whole class teaching more participatory and maximizing the levels of involvement. Despite the strong top-down style of curriculum development which prevails at the present time, teachers as professionals are powerful agents of change.

 Spotlight on Good Practice

- **Classroom seating patterns**: Consider alternative seating patterns to encourage greater participation and to signal that this is a point where there are high expectations of involvement. If all the children move to sit on a carpet for whole class teaching, does this become confused with other whole class contexts such as circle time or registration? Try using a seating pattern which is noticeably different. Where children stay at tables, try rearranging who sits at which table for whole class talk. Consider adopting a specific position as teacher during whole class teaching.

- **Physical resources**: Many teachers successfully use available teaching resources during whole class teaching to generate a response from everybody. Individual whiteboards and number fans have been particularly advocated by the National Literacy and Numeracy Strategies and often work very well to include everyone. Other similar possibilities include: using red and blue cards to signal agreement or disagreement with an answer; using a toy (or real!) microphone to signal who should speak; using coloured counters and a central pot and every child must use their counter by offering a response before the end of the session.

- **Minimize the problem of reluctant volunteers**: Avoid the problems of reluctant or unmotivated children opting out of whole class teaching by using alternative ways of orchestrating responses other than the traditional use of hands up. There is a whole range of imaginative ways to do this, but it is important that children feel safe in this environment rather than vulnerable. Strategies which involve a fun element help create a playful atmosphere, and children should always be reassured that it is OK not to have an answer. This can be managed by allowing children to say 'Pass', or to 'Ask a friend' or a similar device for continuing the interactions. Some alternatives to asking for hands up are outlined below:

  - *No hands up*: Operate a no hands up policy and the teacher selects who will answer.
  - *Talking hat*: Exploit the Harry Potter interest and buy or make a large funny hat (wizard's pointed hat; top hat). Put all the children's names in the hat and select names randomly from the Talking Hat.
  - *Number grid*: Draw a grid with as many numbers as there are children in the class. Randomly allocate each child in the class a number, then during whole class teaching, call out numbers to select who answers. Tick off the numbers on the

grid as they are used. Laminating a numbered grid at the start of term and using a chinagraph pencil which can be rubbed out after use is a good way to save time. The idea could be adapted by using characters from stories the class have shared.

- *Number bingo*: A variation on the above. Prepare four number grids which can be displayed easily with numbers randomly distributed across the four grids. Allocate each child a number, but instead of selecting who answers, invite children to volunteer. As they volunteer, their number is ticked off on the relevant grid, until one grid is complete and all the children with numbers on that grid call out 'Bingo'. This could be used with an interactive whiteboard, if available.
- *Buzz session*: The teacher takes lots of responses from individuals in a short time without comment or feedback; the expectation is that everyone will offer a response.

- **Embed alternatives to teacher–whole class interactions within whole class teaching**: There is no reason why the whole class teaching context should remain consistently whole class. Incorporating short bursts of alternative talk opportunities prior to feedback to the whole class can be a very productive way to maintain engagement and to sustain involvement. Often these strategies give children a chance to think about or talk about the topic or idea, and this gives them time to generate responses. Create an expectation that everybody will respond once the teaching returns to the whole class focus.

  - Ask individuals to 'Write down three things that . . .'
  - *Talking partners*: 'Tell the person next to you what you think about . . .'
  - *Time out*: Give children one minute to discuss what they think about a topic, particularly when it is evident that this is something they seem to feel strongly about.

- **Encourage active listening**: The significance of listening in whole class teaching is often overlooked because the emphasis is so often on spoken answers, but encouraging active listening is itself encouraging better participation.

- *Partner reporter*: Following a quick burst of pair work together, one child has to report back what his/her partner thought.
- *Listening triads*: Children work in threes, but two children discuss a topic or problem, and the third has to listen to the dialogue and report back what they said.
- *Spokesperson*: This is a useful way to manage a transition from group work to whole class teaching. During a group task, one child is appointed Spokesperson: during the last two minutes of group work, the group decide on the key points they have discussed and the spokesperson reports back.
- *Thinking time*: Be more deliberate about giving thinking time before taking responses. Tell the class they have 15 seconds (or more as appropriate) to think about what answer they will give.

- **Expert teacher**: Encourage participation by thinking carefully about the kinds of questions, comments and responses you give as teacher.

  - Draw as much as possible on children's own experiences and shared understandings as the bridge to new understanding.
  - Listen to the responses given and be prepared to invite children to extend, elaborate or justify their answers.
  - Encourage child-to-child interactions within whole class teaching by fostering a willingness to listen to and build on each other's contributions. Support this in the early stages by using a physical resource such as a Listening Hat to indicate which children will be expected to respond to other's answers.
  - Use puppets or toys with younger children to stimulate a response, including in-role dialogue.

Conclusion

In the contemporary context, interactive teaching is perhaps an overused word, and it can unwittingly spotlight attention upon the teacher, rather than the learner, or a classroom community of learners. Different perspectives on interaction refer to differing levels of communication: from simple participation in a teacher–child dialogue, to exchanges between participants of a more elaborate nature, to a learning process involving the co-construction of knowledge in a collaborative community. The role of the teacher in whole class teaching is to manage 'sensitive teacher-led but not teacher-dominated discourse' (Hughes and Westgate 1998) which is attentive to the quality of children's involvement and participation in the talk opportunities, and which is intrinsically concerned with what children's responses reveal about their understandings or misunderstandings. This marries well with Alexander's notion of dialogic teaching as 'distinct from the question–answer–tell routines of so-called "interactive" teaching, aiming to be more consistently searching and more genuinely reciprocal and cumulative' (2004: 1). Effective whole class teaching is firstly, inclusive, and secondly, challenging.

4 Questioning and learning

Why do teachers ask questions?

When we ask a question in a classroom, it is rarely an act of intellectual curiosity, nor is it an attempt to find an answer to something we don't know. When a teacher asks a question, as is well understood by children, she already knows the answer or a range of possible answers. The child's response therefore is measured against this expectation. While teachers may be open to having expectations challenged, the rules of classroom interaction frequently dictate that the child is looking for a particular answer: the one in the teacher's head. In this sense the teacher's question might be perceived as a straitjacket. Through questioning, the teacher controls the discourse, framing suitable questions and deciding on acceptable answers. The encouragement for teachers to ask open questions (Barnes *et al.* 1986) is in part concerned with breaking down the restriction conferred when some answers are deemed to be better than others and the best answers of all are the ones the teacher is expecting. Kirby (1996: 9) argues, in the context of reading, that the role of the teacher as the questioner in the classroom teaches the child that their own knowledge 'is subordinate to the text and the teacher'. This view of teacher questioning positions children as passive vessels into which the knowledge of the teachers is poured. In contrast, Hargreaves *et al.* (2002) see questioning as an inclusive strategy, enabling children to be active learners. They equate questions with interactivity and statements with transmission. Thus the ratio of statements to questions can be an indicator of the extent to which classroom discourse is teacher-dominated or participatory. For the teachers involved in the TALK project, questioning was less a means of controlling the lesson content, and more a means of scaffolding learning. They attributed considerable significance to questioning, believing that it encouraged children to be more engaged, allowed teachers to monitor what was

---

Box 4.1 Teachers' voices

- Questioning is a strategy which allows 'children to be more active in their learning'.
- 'A means of assessing children's existing knowledge and as a means of reviewing what they had learnt from the previous session'.
- 'By questioning how or why things work, children can develop their thinking and are not just trying to give the right answer.'

---

understood, and gave children opportunities to rehearse ideas and develop their thinking.

The teachers' views reflected a consensus that good questioning increased the interactivity of teaching and the quality of children's learning. The key perspectives on questioning held by these teachers are outlined below:

- Questioning is a way of involving children.
- Open questions are superior to closed questions.
- Good questions are the tools of the trade for effective teaching.
- The best questions facilitate learning and thinking.

With this in mind, we set about analysing the teachers' questions from the video recordings of our participating teachers. What would be the features of an effective question? Which questions would encourage engagement and interactivity and which would close it down? Which questions would allow children to develop their thinking? Do some questions act as scaffolds, while others act as straitjackets?

You might think it would be a straightforward task to begin analysis by separating the questions from the statements. It became clear, however, that a statement such as 'Tell me what you know about multiplying by 10' was as much a question as the grammatically constructed question 'Have you got a pencil?' and rather more probing. We took the decision from the outset, therefore, that any question or statement that invited a response would be defined as a question. This would capture all those genuine attempts on the part of the teacher to involve the children in the talk. Our early attempts to recognize 'open' and 'closed' questions also proved problematic as the terms seemed to be as much defined by the children's responses to the questions as by the nature of the questions themselves. So when a Year 2 teacher asked, 'What is spring?' the subsequent responses from the children suggest they believed they were responding to an open question:

Jane:	When the flowers come out.
David:	When the leaves fall off the trees.
Teacher:	Well, that's autumn – in spring the new shoots start to grow.
Jamie:	It's a little bit cold and a little bit hot.
Teacher:	That's a lovely description of spring.
Sarah:	The daffodils come out.

But the teacher's next comment reveals she was actually asking a closed question with one answer in mind, which she gives them when none of their answers match up:

Teacher: Yes, they do, that's right . . . well, spring is a season.

It was clear we were going to require a more sophisticated model than merely comparing statements to questions, or open with closed questions. Analysing the huge variety of questions asked by these teachers, identifying what kinds of questions they were, and establishing their purpose was further complicated by the way in which children answered these questions. We wanted to capture this complexity.

What kinds of questions do teachers ask?

The process of allowing the coding structure for the questions to emerge as we coded has been outlined in Chapter 2, as has our decision to code not only for the form the questions took, but also for the subtle ways in which questions were used. So we ascribed both a form and a function to every question. Table 4.1 defines the four question forms we identified, together with examples of questions coded as having this form.

Table 4.1   The categorization of the form of the question

Form	Definition	Example
Factual	Questions inviting a predetermined answer	*What do I have to mix to make green?* *What is 5 plus 5?* *Why do plants have flowers?*
Speculative	Questions inviting a response with no predetermined answer, often opinions, hypotheses, imaginings, ideas	*Anyone have any ideas what that could mean?* *Do you think zoos are a good idea?* *Anyone have any opinions about those three children?* *If I made the slope higher, what do you think might happen then?*
Process	Questions inviting children to articulate their understanding of learning processes/explain their thinking	*How did you work that out?* *How do you know that?* *Can you explain why?*
Procedural	Questions relating to the organization and management of the lesson	*Can you all see?*

Simply categorizing questions for form would not have highlighted the more three-dimensional picture that recognized how questions operate within whole class interaction. From this perspective, it is not a matter of good questions and bad questions, but more about the right question at the right moment. There will be times when a snappy factual question that establishes basic principles is precisely what is required and when the more open-ended speculative questions slow the pace down inappropriately. There may be times when a statement achieves more than a question can. If you have a key word in your head, it might be easier to state it clearly, rather than to spend time heavily cueing questions in order to elicit it from the children.

Comparing the three factual questions given in Table 4.1 we can identify that although they are all factual questions, they serve a different function. 'What do I have to do to mix green?' has the function of eliciting factual information and at a particular moment in an art lesson it might be all that is required to progress the thinking. The mathematical question 'What is 5 plus 5?' is concerned with practising the skill of addition. For some children this will be a question of recall, for others it will involve using addition skills to compute the answer. All questions that practise skills will demand a varying degree of thought depending both on the difficulty of the question and on the ability of the child. So while such questions are clearly closed questions, having a single possible answer, and also factual questions, they may require higher-order thinking skills to resolve them. The question about why plants have flowers is from a science lesson looking at seeds and required the children to make explicit their thinking as to the connection between flowers and seeds, encouraging them to build on their thinking. It is an example of the teacher consciously attempting to move the children's thinking forward and encouraging them to link ideas together. While this question might be seen as drawing more on higher-order thinking skills than the other two, what makes it a 'good' question is the context from which it comes. A question of this sort needs to come at a point in the lesson when the children have been supported enough to make the cognitive link. In the light of these subtleties, Table 4.2 defines the 11 functions of questions that we identified.

Having categorized the questions both for the form they took and the function they fulfilled, we were able to consider what patterns of questioning characterized whole class teaching. Previous research, as we explored in Chapter 1, had repeatedly found that we tend to use a lot of factual questions in teaching at the expense of more speculative or reasoning questions which solicit higher-level thinking. All previous research however had predated the introduction of the National Literacy and Numeracy Strategies and the changed emphasis on whole class teaching, and we were interested to see if this had altered the nature of questions used. It hadn't! As you can see in Table 4.3, the pattern of heavy use of factual questioning remains as dominant a tendency as it has always been. Over 60 per cent of all questions asked were factual. Teachers' questions thus appear to be more concerned with asking children to tell them the 'right' answer, rather than with thinking and speculating. When we compared the ratio of questions to statements in the whole sample, statements predominated at a ratio of 3: 2, another sign that the teaching is predisposed to telling and transmitting information. A crude caricature

Table 4.2 The categorization of the function of the question

Function of question	Definition
Class management	Related to management of behaviour/tasks
Factual elicitation	Asking for recall of fact/information
Cued elicitation	Giving clues to answer
Building on content	Gathering information about the topic/theme
Building on thinking	Making children think about the ideas and concepts; this moves ideas forward, unlike the checking understanding, which looks back at ideas already covered
Recapping	Recalling past lessons and work done in this lesson
Practising skills	Inviting children to rehearse, repeat or practise a strategy or grasp of understanding
Checking prior knowledge	Checking child's knowledge and experience which might be relevant to lesson
Developing vocabulary	Testing or clarifying understanding of words
Checking understanding	Querying understanding and checking grasp of learning undertaken
Developing reflection	Inviting children to think about how they are learning and the strategies they are using

Table 4.3 The categorization of questions by form

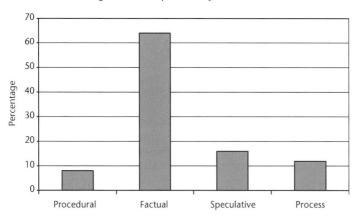

of this pattern would be teachers telling children lots of facts and asking children to recall lot of those facts.

But this is indeed a crude caricature. By categorizing the function of questions as well as the form, a different light is cast on the teachers' questions (see Table 4.4). It remains true that the most common function was factual elicitation, a lower level recall skill, but that 17 per cent of questions sought to build on thinking is much more encouraging, as are those questions that practise skills, develop vocabulary, check understanding, check prior knowledge, and develop reflection. A significant proportion of the questions, including the factual questions, were functioning in a way that was supportive of children's learning.

So not all factual questions are bad questions, and the decision to code questions both for form and function reveals a much more sophisticated picture of the teacher's use of talk, one that is not entirely depressing and one that spotlights existing practice from which lessons can be drawn and new strategies developed. Nevertheless, the fact that speculative and process questions, which involve higher-order thinking processes, account for only 28 per cent of all questions, and that a third of all factual questions were indeed either heavily cued to a 'right' answer or eliciting a 'right' answer, points to a clear area for further development.

Furthermore the video transcripts of the lessons from which this data was gleaned reveals that the dominant discourse pattern was

Table 4.4 The categorization of the questions by function

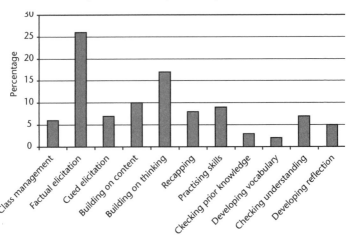

teacher–child–teacher–child, rather like a ping pong game, with each teacher utterance filling a paragraph while each child utterance barely filled a line. Very rarely was this pattern disrupted with a pattern such as teacher–child–child–child–teacher. In general, children's answers served to end an interaction pattern, and very rarely to begin or extend it. Indeed, the low significance that was sometimes given to children's answers exemplified how conversations were at times prevented in pursuit of some notional right answer. In several instances, the category for a question was determined by the way the teacher handled the child's response, as is demonstrated by the following example. This comes from a Year 6 RE lesson and the teacher is discussing the role of the imam within the Islamic community.

> *Teacher:*   Can you remember anything else? One thing that we've said most religious leaders would do, it wouldn't matter what religion they were leading. The vicar does it, the rabbi does it.

While this is a factual question, its function could certainly be to develop factual understanding about religious practices. Alternatively, the question could develop thinking at a more abstract level about the idea of ministry and the role of the laity and the ordained, or similarities and differences in practices between different faiths. But a clue that the teacher has only one answer in mind is intimated by the 'one thing' in her question. In the interactional sequence initiated by this question, several children make plausible responses, all of which are redirected back towards the 'real' answer that the teacher has in her head. The first response offered is from Jason:

> They do things like services.

While this is a perfectly sensible response from Jason, it is not, unfortunately, the answer the teacher is after. If it was, then the conversation would have ended here. The teacher struggles on, giving a heavy clue, the phrase 'another thing' again suggesting there is a particular answer in mind:

> Yes, but there was another thing that we said religious leaders would go round and do.

Thus prompted by 'go round', Dawn suggests:

> Going round when people are ill.

Now the conversation is moving in the direction the teacher wants and so her input encourages conversation along these lines:

> Yes, perhaps an old person or a family where someone had died.

At this point, the conversation becomes distracted from the intended theme, 'concern for the community', by Lucy who offers the observation that:

> He can't get all emotional himself.

The comment is accepted and developed by the teacher, but ultimately her input turns the talk back to the teacher agenda:

> Right. He's got to be able to detach himself, by that I mean not get all sitting there and sobbing, but he's got to, at the same time, what . . .?

Adam contributes:

> Be calm.

This is closer to the required answer, and the teacher prompts a further response by her use of 'and also' and finally gets the answer she wanted all along:

> *Teacher:* Calm and also . . .
> *Adam:* Concerned.
> *Teacher:* Concerned, caring, show that he's concerned.

In some respects, this became a conversation because the teacher did not get the answer she was looking for; it almost became an interesting conversation but for the need to return to the teacher's agenda of eliciting the single acceptable response to her initial factual question. It is far too easy to denigrate teachers through examples like this and suggest incompetent practice, but this is counter to the spirit of the TALK project and of this book. It's likely that almost everyone who has ever been engaged in teaching activity at any level has led an interaction sequence like this. Like asking leading questions in an interview, it is a pitfall of questioning which is stimulated by the desire to support and to achieve the intended goal. It may be impossible to eliminate this kind of sequence from teaching, but the important professional issue is to develop awareness of it happening, and to try and deploy strategies which minimize its likelihood (see the *Spotlight on Good Practice* at the end of this chapter). The question itself however also demonstrates how many questions have the potential to draw on higher-order thinking skills, intentionally or otherwise. There is as much skill in handling the children's answers as there is in composing the perfect question.

Box 4.2   Talking point

- Do we really listen to the answers children offer?
- Is there a difference between a question that facilitates teaching and one that facilitates learning?
- Are there key questions that will elicit improved responses?
- Is there a place for preplanning our questions?
- Do we think about why we ask questions?

Taking a closer look

When we look at the patterns of questioning in different age groups and different curriculum areas, further subtleties and complexities emerge. Year 6 teachers, for example, asked almost twice as many process questions as Year 2 teachers, and asked more questions that built on thinking and reflected on learning. It is possible that this reflects a greater emphasis on the concrete rather than the abstract in early years' classrooms. More curiously, almost all of the questions that checked for prior knowledge were asked by Year 2 teachers. The teachers involved suggested that more limited acknowledgement of prior knowledge in Year 6 could be attributable to the approaching Key Stage 2 tests. These might account for different priorities in Year 6 whereby what is needed to be known becomes more important than what is known already. The greatest differences between patterns of questioning however occur not between age groups but between the curriculum areas. The process question was most likely to be found in the numeracy lesson, while the speculative question was most likely to be found in literacy and other subjects:

Table 4.5 Patterns of questioning in numeracy and literacy

Examples of Process questions in numeracy	Examples of Speculative questions in literacy
• How did you get to that answer?	• Give me some reasons why the elephant might be frightened?
• Did anybody do it differently?	• When might you want to use that kind of sense of mystery?
• What strategy did you use?	• What would happen if somebody built a huge leisure centre right in my front garden?
• How do you know that half of 500 is 250?	• What would be the negative things that could happen?

In numeracy, the ratio of process questions to speculative questions was 4: 1 while in literacy this ratio is reversed in favour of speculative questions. This pattern is also reflected in the function of the questions, so while very few questions in numeracy build on thinking, the greatest number of examples of questions with the function of reflecting on learning come from numeracy lessons, with the reverse being true for literacy and other subjects. Almost all the examples of practising skills come from numeracy lessons. This pattern of questioning in numeracy suggests not only a subject-specific discourse for mathematical understanding, which prioritizes processes and functions over factual information, but also teachers' recognition that understanding how to tackle a mathematical problem is more important than arriving at the correct answer, and that teacher talk and questioning has to enable this kind of thinking. It may also reflect some of the emphasis of the National Numeracy Strategy and its encouragement to create opportunities for children to practise skills, and to invite children 'to demonstrate and explain their methods and reasoning, and explore reasons for any wrong answers' (DfEE 1999a: 5). Indeed, a recent Ofsted review of the numeracy strategy draws explicit attention to the importance of 'effective questioning to encourage pupils to explain their calculations' (Ofsted 2002: 9). Teachers' questioning in numeracy foregrounds this kind of thinking, with questions typically framed in 'How do you . . .' and 'Why do you . .' formats.

This questioning pattern deriving from numeracy could well strengthen thinking and learning in literacy, through the use of process questions such as 'How do you know it is a verb?' or 'How can you tell she is scared?' Two of the participating teachers investigated the use of process questions in literacy as a follow-up to the TALK project through the Best Practice Research Scholarships. One of these teachers observed the efficacy of the process question in numeracy and the way in which it allowed the teacher to follow a child's reasoning in arriving at a certain answer. In her planning for literacy lessons, she began to think of certain literacy skills in terms of the thinking processes required, particularly in relation to spelling and punctuation. She noted process questions she might legitimately use within the context of the lesson and created opportunities to ask them. Her reflections on this strategy was that it not only helped her to understand what a child knew, but helped a child to understand both what she knew and how she knew it.

Box 4.3   Teachers' voices

- 'Children have been able to recall methods used to work out spellings when reading and writing and have become aware of the reasons for using punctuation.'
- She used 'drama and invitations to empathize with characters in stories, for example, by showing how we know they are happy or sad.'
- 'If children are encouraged to develop thinking skills and verbalize "how" and "why" they know something, they will be able to confidently draw upon these skills in future and become more independent learners.'

Children's voices

From the 54 lessons observed and recorded, there were only 20 examples of children asking questions, meaning that in the majority of lessons observed there were no questions from children at all. Children's voices in general and their questioning voices in particular are rather silent in our whole class 'interactive' teaching. It becomes important, therefore, not only to frame questions in such a way that children's participation is increased, but to consider how well we listen and respond to their answers. Allowing children more time to respond to questions increases the length of response the child is likely to offer (Rowe 1996). Waiting before you take an answer implies that you expect a thoughtful response rather than an instant one and gives the children thinking time. By increasing wait times, you also buy yourselves thinking time to listen and respond to what children say.

It is possible to construct two contrasting pictures of how children's voices are received and encouraged within our classrooms; neither picture is complete but both reflect the patterns of questioning that have been observed. The first is the classroom where children's talk merely fills in the missing words. The teacher's agenda and lesson planning dominates the talk, and the talk delivers the content of the lesson with the occasional pause for a child to offer brief answers to questions operating as a verbal 'cloze procedure'. In contrast is the classroom where children's talk is given space and in which the child's answers actually matter. They matter because they reveal a child's thinking and understanding, or misunderstanding. The teacher's response to the child reflects this, either by moving the thinking forward or by addressing the misunderstanding. The child's answer might change the focus of the lesson, either because old learning has to be revisited or because the child's response creates opportunities not anticipated in the teacher's planning. Whilst the second classroom scenario is clearly a more constructive learning environment, the existence of the first classroom scenario is influenced by tensions between conflicting imperatives to balance curriculum coverage with classroom opportunity and spontaneity. The teachers involved in the TALK project were well aware of this dilemma; they voiced a strong belief that the demands of the National Literacy Strategy required them not only to prioritize coverage, but to deliver it in a certain way. The NLS emphasis on 'well-paced' teaching with a 'sense of urgency' (DfEE 1998: 8) may actively encourage factual, closed questioning, because these questions occupy the least time. Pace and factual quick-fire questions may well have become synonymous. Giving children the floor not only slows the pace, but also risks the teacher losing control over the content and objectives of the lesson. There is, therefore, a strong incentive to keep children's contributions brief and focused, rather than opening up thinking, reasoning and explaining through questioning.

Spotlight on Good Practice

- **Increase the variety of questions asked:**

  - Ask fewer factual questions and more higher-order questions that invite speculation, hypothesis and analysis.
  - If it is more natural to generate factual questions when you think on your feet, then actively preplan some questions that promote thinking about concepts or allow for the expressing of a personal response.
  - Ask more 'How do you know that?' or 'Why do you think that?' questions.
  - Ask provocative questions that invite disagreement and debate.
  - Find opportunities to ask genuine questions in which the answer matters because you don't know it already. Allow yourself to be the non-expert. 'I don't understand, can you explain?' or ask questions that you and the children, or the children in groups or pairs have to work together to resolve.
  - Help the children to understand that not all questions are the same. Explain what terms such as speculate, reflect and wonder mean. Then plan times when you and the child, or the children in pairs or groups speculate or reflect together.
  - Consider how the same content can generate different kinds of questions:

What is a verb?	Factual question
If a verb is a doing word, why is 'sleeping' a verb?	Speculative question
How can you tell which word is the verb in this sentence?	Process question

- **Improve the appropriateness of questions asked:**

  - Publish the challenging or the key questions in a display mode, and refer back to them.
  - Having identified your key questions, can you answer them yourself? Sometimes what seems like a good question is not quite as appropriate as you think when you try to answer it.

- Don't assume your question will elicit the response you expect. Imagine and anticipate the variety of responses your key question might prompt and consider how you will handle them.
- After asking a factual question and receiving the expected answer, ask children if there were any alternative answers or different ways of considering the question.
- Reflect upon the way you use questions, the type of questions you ask and when you ask them. Do you always start lessons with statements and/or factual questions or do you prefer to start with speculative questions? Try stopping and thinking before you ask a question, and identify its purpose at this point of this lesson. Different types of questions tend to prompt different kinds of responses:

  factual questions elicit predetermined answers – recall of facts, content and possible knowledge;

  speculative questions target ideas and hypotheses;

  procedural questions are appropriate for class management and clear explanations or task setting;

  process questions enable children to explain what they are thinking and understanding.

- Consider whether a lesson you are about to teach will be mainly:

  exposition – explaining and presenting content;

  discussion – conversations around a topic;

  skill learning – demonstrating and practising a skill;

  investigative – experimenting.

Then choose your question type appropriately to match the purpose of the teaching.

- If you want to convey facts, consider if questioning is really necessary. There are other alternatives such as telling, suggesting, negotiating, thinking aloud.

- **Encourage children's voices:**

  - When asking a question, remember to stop and listen to the response. Listen to the children's answers before framing the next questions and adapt your questioning if necessary.

- Lengthen the wait time before taking answers.
- Create opportunities for children to ask questions: preparing interviews; coming up with three questions they want to ask you about a topic; writing down a question about something they don't understand; devising questions in pairs for other pairs to answer.
- Try following a speculative question from which a variety of responses were elicited with group talk, in which the children come up with the five best answers and why they have selected these five.
- If you are recapping on previous learning for the whole class, consider whether individual questioning of children is going to give you the information you are seeking. It might be more effective for groups of children to work together to explain what they learned previously to each other – the task could be to come up with one good question to ask another group to test pupils' knowledge. This activity might only take two or three minutes and could be more effective in refreshing more memories than the individually targeted recall question.

Conclusion

The dominance of the factual question might suggest that teachers all too often give in to the incentive to keep children's contributions brief in order to maintain pace and focus. The TALK project, however, revealed that teachers used a variety of questioning strategies. There was evidence that a single lesson might include short bursts of factual questions to begin a lesson, followed by questions that check understanding, from which teachers might establish a base from which to develop thinking. Other teachers began with open questions and used the children's answers to move the thinking forward. Teachers' questions altered depending on the context, such as their place within the lesson, the age of the children being taught, and the subject being taught. Merely comparing one kind of question with another does not do justice to the skills of teachers in judging the appropriateness of the question to its context. Nevertheless, what is revealed here is the need to assess if the factual question is overused, and how teachers might use a greater variety of questions that elicit more elaborate, developed and thoughtful responses from children.

Teachers have to balance the need to manage classroom behaviour, while pursuing the lesson aims, as well as creating opportunities for up to 30 children to experience meaningful talk that develops their thinking and encourages them to reflect on their learning. This is talk that by its very nature may be slow, tentative and exploratory, requiring sensitive and imaginative handling from the teacher. That it is often successful and engaging is testimony to the skill of classroom teachers.

connections. Equally, it is very easy to make assumptions that children's prior knowledge is present, and plan teaching on this foundation, when actually some or all of the children do not have the requisite knowledge. On reflection, after a lesson using interview as a way of generating talk, one teacher in the TALK project realized that she had made an incorrect assumption: 'I wanted the children to interview each other in pairs. I had assumed their understanding of the word "interview" – how wrong I was!' In a Year 2 science lesson, looking at flowers, seeds and germination, the teacher was using a broad bean seed as a focus for thinking about what conditions seeds need to grow, and about half way through the teaching, one child piped up and asked 'Miss, what is a broad bean?' In both cases the assumption of prior knowledge meant that children were puzzled and confused about the tasks they had to do. In both cases, however, the gap in prior knowledge was revealed because one teacher was reflecting on her teaching and became aware of the difficulty, and the other teacher had created an atmosphere where children were sufficiently confident to reveal their own lack of understanding.

An exciting feature of young children's minds is that they do appear to naturally seek to make connections between their experiences and understandings, even if as teachers we do not always pick up on them. We are often more aware of this as parents, where we are in the more fortunate position of dealing with only two or three sets of understandings rather than 30. Wells (1986) found that parents extended children's thinking, attempted to understand their comments and misunderstandings, and helped establish connections far more than teachers did. This positions children differently in terms of responsibility for achieving an understanding as Wood (1988) notes: for preschool children adults take the responsibility for working out what the child means, but in school the child has to work out what the adult means. I remember a former Devon Adviser for English illustrating how learning to read is about making connections between the text and life knowledge by telling a story about his son. During a walk round a National Trust garden, they went through a wooden gate with a notice saying 'Beware of the creosote'. The child asked his father to read the sign, which he did, and they continued the walk. That evening, the boy was drawing a picture of a monster and when the father asked him what he was drawing, the boy replied 'It's a creosote!' He had, entirely reasonably and plausibly, made connections between signs on gates saying 'Beware of the dog', the sign on the creosote-painted gate, and his story knowledge of monsters and the need to be wary of them. Because of the one-to-one relationship of father and son, and the common experience of going out for a walk, the father developed an understanding of how his son was thinking.

This kind of shared understanding, or 'mutuality of perspective' (Edwards and Mercer 1987: 1) is central to effective learning in the classroom. Making connections between prior knowledge and new learning, or between the given and the new, is a complex and multi-faceted process, and on their own, children may well make undeveloped or even inaccurate connections, and thus never acquire what Edwards and Mercer call 'principled understanding' (1987: 95), which is rooted in meaningful, conceptual understanding rather than superficial connections. The role of talk is pivotal in fostering principled understanding through establishing meaningful connections between the given and the new. First, for the child articulating what he or she knows or understands is part of the process of learning: talk is not simply repeating aloud preformed thoughts in the head; rather it 'structures and directs the processes of thinking and concept formation' (Wood 1988: 29). In other words, talk is the means of making connections. Second, a child's talk is a mirror of his or her understanding, and so it allows us to see the kinds of connections

---

Box 5.1   Teachers' voices

- I was pleased that I gave a chance for several children to talk about their previous knowledge of the word. All the contributions added something to the children's understanding of the word. Emily related the meaning of the word to her own ideas about maths – the rich people are the tens and the peasants are the ones, twos and zeros.
- I asked the children when they had heard the word average used before. I felt that for those children who had previous experience of the term, this talk may have developed their understanding of how the term could be used in the lesson context. In particular the example raised by a child of when they had looked at average results in science provided a prompt for the other children.
- The talk at the start of the session I think is useful – it gives children the chance to recap on, and talk through or explain their understanding of what they already know before moving forward.

which are being made, and to build upon those to establish principled understanding.

Making connections through talk

If talk is one of the principal ways in which we can make connections between children's prior knowledge and the new learning being developed, then it is important to consider *how* talk is used to achieve this. Mercer observed teachers working with children and categorized how talk was used to link the present to the past to establish understanding. He suggested that there are five teacher strategies at our disposal:

- Recap – brief review of earlier experiences;
- Elicitation – usually to draw out information;
- Repetition – repeating what a child says either to confirm or question the response;
- Reformulation – paraphrase;
- Exhortation – 'try and remember' questions asking for recall.

(Mercer 2000: 52)

Most teachers use all of these techniques at some point in their teaching, although there is variety both in how and how much they are used. In Table 5.1 we have collected examples from different lessons and different teachers to illustrate each of Mercer's five strategies.

Reading through the examples in Table 5.1 you might have noticed that many of them come from the start of a lesson, as this tended to be the most common point at which to address prior knowledge. The analysis of the video data, however, revealed that accessing and using children's prior knowledge was not a strong feature of teachers' interactions with children during whole class talk. Recapping was the most frequently used strategy, with 9 per cent of teacher statements and 8 per cent of teacher questions being used to recap. Statements that drew on prior knowledge and questions which elicited prior knowledge were even fewer, at 3 per cent and 2 per cent respectively.

Because whole class teaching tends to adopt a pattern of teacher–child–teacher–child interactions, it can be difficult to give sufficient time to addressing the varying levels of prior knowledge in the class.

Table 5.1   Mercers' five strategies with examples from the TALK project

Recap	*Year 2 PSHE* Here I have again those funny letters that we had last week in RE and PSHE, because we're going to continue with what we started last week. Because in that time together we found out that I belonged to a football club.
	Year 6 Literacy I've left yesterday's objective up, which was to identify key events as a basis for telling the story. What we're going to do today is to write about some of those key events, so it's kind of linked.
	Year 4 Numeracy Right, you remember that last week we said we were going to try different kinds of multiplication. Right, so we're going to go first over things that we know a bit about and then we're going to move on to do some new kinds of multiplication.
Elicitation	*Year 3 History* What's special about Henry VIII? Anyone know anything special about King Henry VIII?
Repetition	*Year 2 Literacy* *Teacher:* Yesterday we looked at a poem; who can remember what the poem was about? *Sarah:* Going barefeet. *Teacher:* Going barefeet. Where were we going barefeet? *Joe:* To the beach. *Teacher:* To the beach. Anything else you can remember about that poem?
	Year 3 History *Teacher:* We're going to come together to study history; can anyone tell me what history is? *Jake:* It's things that are in the past *Teacher:* Things that are in the past. That's a good answer. What sort of things would you regard as history then? *Lee:* World War II. *Teacher:* World War II. *Emma:* Ancient Egypt. *Teacher:* Yes, Ancient Egypt – we'll come back to that. Anything else that you would say was history?

Sam: The Fire of London.

Teacher: The Fire of London, we did that last year, didn't we?

Reformulation *Year 6 Literacy*

Stacey: I had an argument with my friend because she was going out to a party and she came out and she'd just bought this new white top and I accidentally spilt blackcurrant on it.

Teacher: And you had an argument about it, a big argument? So a big argument could be stemming from ruining something. Maxine?

Maxine: I had a massive argument with my stepdad when Naomi came round, and it was really embarrassing because . . . and I got really upset and started shouting.

Teacher: So . . . go on.

Maxine: She started teasing me and I was really embarrassed.

Teacher: So we're saying an argument could come from a time when you've been really embarrassed by somebody or when you've damaged something that belongs to someone else.

Exhortation *Year 4 Maths*

First of all can you remember why we said yesterday that the lattice method worked well but the Romans didn't do much multiplication. Why was it? Why was it that the Romans didn't do multiplication very much?

An alternative is to shift to pair talk briefly, and then return to the whole class teaching, like the Year 3 teacher in our project who began a history lesson by asking the children to talk together in pairs about what they had discussed in the previous history lesson. The buzz that this created was in evident contrast to the more usual pattern of children listening to the teacher and answering, recapping questions in turn. Another situation, which draws on prior knowledge and generates lively and animated talk, is when children are given the opportunity to talk about their experiences in connection with the classroom learning. A Year 6 class who were reading Roald Dahl's *Boy* were asked to think about incidents in their own lives that might make interesting autobiographical accounts. In the flow of responses

Box 5.2 Talking point
• How often do you try to draw on children's prior knowledge in your whole class teaching?   • Is there any difference between prior knowledge and prior experience?   • Which of Mercer's five strategies do you tend to use the most?

which followed, it was noticeable that children's responses were longer and more extended than usual, as in the example from Luke below:

> Um, me and Jamie was making a swing at the end of the close, and then I got up in the tree and he got up in the tree and I started jumping on the branch, and he was sitting on it and he swinged round and I stamped on the branch really hard and the branch snapped and I went with the branch and landed on Jamie's head [children laugh].

Prior knowledge – an issue of time and curriculum coverage?

When you read the examples of teacher strategies for linking prior knowledge and present learning in the table earlier in this chapter, you might have noticed that the majority of the examples made a connection which was essentially school-focused. One unfortunate impact of national strategies in literacy and numeracy, and of systems such as Ofsted and league tables, which make teachers and schools very aware of accountability, may have been to make teachers more focused on what they need to teach, rather than what children need to learn. It was very evident in the TALK project that teachers conceptualized prior knowledge in terms of making connections over time between one aspect of curriculum coverage and another, as the quotations below reveal:

• In previous lessons the children had worked on using interesting verbs. The previous week they had been using simple and complex sentences.

- We were revisiting force which is introduced in their earlier education and also requires some general knowledge . . . The use of standard and non-standard measuring has been the most revisited knowledge.
- Work in previous two years at school; previous cross-curricular work . . . work on tadpoles done in previous two weeks.
- Building on lessons from last term; work on data handling in Year 5.
- Year 5 work on area; Year 6 work.
- Children had done some doubling. I was reinforcing and introducing the times two element.
- We had previously explored bias and how it is necessary to see both sides . . . We had also spent some time exploring language and how the type of text governs the choice of vocabulary.

This association of prior knowledge with curriculum coverage in a school context may also account for the emphasis on recapping as the principal strategy for drawing on children's prior knowledge. Recapping involves teachers telling or asking children what they have done previously, and it is very controlled by the teacher, giving relatively little space for children's own thinking. Many recapping questions are factual questions, requiring recall, but not necessarily understanding. During the TALK project, the teachers became increasingly aware of this, including one teacher who realized that her own way of thinking about prior knowledge was limited to curriculum coverage: 'I think I fell into the "trap" of believing this to mean "re-capping" on what had occurred in previous lessons rather than "prior knowledge"!'

It's worth considering children's own perspectives on prior knowledge, particularly how they see the connections and inter-relationships between what they learn in school and out of school. When children in the TALK project were interviewed after their lessons, we asked them if they knew anything already about the topic or skill the lesson had addressed. Perhaps not surprisingly, like their teachers, they were more likely to talk about prior knowledge based on previous curriculum coverage than in relation to out-of-school learning or experience, as the following comments indicate:

- When we were in Year 1 with Miss James.

- We had already done it in Year 5. Because we didn't have much to do we learnt a bit more about it.
- We did it last year.
- We did some in Year 5 but not much about decimals. It was just like halves and that, and quarters, and that's all we know.
- I've known adding because of Year 1, but I haven't known multiply.
- I knew how to do the bits about the argument and we'd learnt a little bit about formal writing.
- In maths sets before we learned about the mode, the medium, the range, and the mean, and we'd learnt a bit about how to add up and the difference of decimals quickly.

It does seem that many children may be separating what they learn in school from other learning, which limits and narrows the possibilities for making relevant interconnections in their learning. There were some examples of children making sense of what they were doing in school in the light of home experience, like Carla in Year 2 who made a connection between mathematical divisions and her social experience of sharing: 'I share out some of my sweets with my brother and sister.' Similarly, Tom in Year 6 recognized that the learning focus of the lesson was 'how to put both points of view down to make a balanced discussion' which linked with his television viewing of the House of Commons in action: 'Sometimes I saw it on TV where they have – in the House of thing – and they have conversations sometimes' (though we might question whether this is balanced discussion).

One curious feature to emerge from interviewing the children was the pattern that low-achieving boys seemed to be considerably more likely than any other group to refer to out-of-school personal experience and prior knowledge; low-achieving boys were also more likely to try and move conversations on to their own agenda. The graphs in Table 5.2 illustrate this pattern.

Given national concern about boys' achievement and about boys' engagement with school, this could be a significant issue and well worth exploring in the context of your own classroom. The nature of the low-achieving boys' response to classroom learning suggests that they may be more inclined to learn by drawing on their own experiences and by reacting to learning introduced through personal and unconventional responses. It may be that they are less tuned in to the culture of school and schooled ways of working than

Table 5.2 How low-achieving and high-achieving boys and girls made reference to prior knowledge

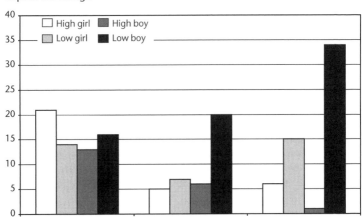

their peers, and particularly less so than high-achieving girls who appear to be more in harmony with the teacher than other groups. Like the teachers, high-achieving girls conceive of prior knowledge as predominantly about school experience, and they recall more facts from the lesson and understand lesson purposes more clearly than others. It may be that explicitly making more use of boys' out-of-school learning, interests and experiences could help them become more focused and engaged with in-school learning.

Prior knowledge: building cognitive connections

Rather than thinking about curriculum coverage and topical or thematic links with previous work, it is more constructive to think about prior knowledge in terms of building blocks of thinking and understanding, so that children start to link underlying principles or concepts, not just topics. Although their conceptualizing of children's prior knowledge seemed strongly curriculum and school focused, the teachers involved in the TALK project were very clear about the learning they wished to address in their lessons and were clear themselves about some of the cognitive connections they hoped to create (Box 5.3).

Box 5.3 Teachers' voices

- The children had had much experience of shared writing activities and of producing their own narrative. They were familiar with starting their sentences in different ways, using participles, adjectives, connectives etc. They had used dialogue effectively and knew the correct layout. They had on many occasions in the past experimented with vocabulary and enjoyed improving on shared writing.
- Evidence of previous work on effective story writing was evident. They knew how they could begin the narrative, e.g. with action or speech. One child suggested dialogue should come next and another noted that the description was limited and needed developing.
- I was building on their knowledge of U × U and of their multiplication tables, on a previous introduction to the grid methods of multiplication, and on doubling and halving, partitioning and odd and even numbers.
- When discussing with someone whether their answer would be the same if they reversed the order in which they used the numbers for the multiplication, I asked them 'Do you normally get the same answer if you reverse two numbers in multiplication?' to use their prior knowledge.

If children could not think of a previous time in school when they had covered the topic or a related one, they were very likely to say they knew nothing about it all; this may of course be absolutely true, as each lesson is developing something new and unfamiliar, but it may be useful to try to support children explicitly in making cognitive connections which they are missing. For example, following a Year 2 science lesson on seeds which used a poppy as an example, Sarah remembered that they had grown sunflowers from seeds in Year 1, 'but I didn't know anything about poppies'. She is making a connection between flower type, rather than seed characteristics, which is getting in the way of her learning about seeds. Sometimes these connections can be made very directly at the start of a lesson, like the Year 4 teacher who began her numeracy lesson by linking previous learning with the learning about to be tackled, building up their grasp of multiplication:

> Right, you remember that last week we said we were going to try different kinds of multiplication. Right, so we're going to go first over things that we know a bit about and then we're going to move on to do some new kinds of multiplication. So today we're thinking about partitioning large numbers to make multiplying easier.

More often building cognitive connections relies less on planning and more on effective listening to children's comments and responses. With 30 children and a sense of pressure and accountability to achieve predetermined learning objectives, it is very easy to miss responses that reveal some relevant prior knowledge but that are not directly related to the learning focus. In a Year 3 history lesson exploring burial rituals, the teacher explains that burial rituals have evolved because 'when someone dies you have to do something with the body because they don't need it any more', and she tells the class that today we either bury or cremate bodies because leaving bodies lying around to rot would be unpleasant. One child picks up on the burial/cremation choice and draws on some prior knowledge of the environmental issues relating to the waste of land with burial and cemeteries. She tells the teacher 'I know why they are burned, because the more they are buried, the more they'll take up loads of land', but the teacher only gives this passing acknowledgement and redirects them back to her teaching focus: 'Oh so, that's a thought. So a burial ritual is what you do to dispose of the body.' This is a missed opportunity to incorporate this prior knowledge and cognitive connection into the lesson, and to validate the child's contribution.

Sensitive listening to children's responses to hear what it tells us about their prior knowledge and underlying thinking is also important in addressing misconceptions or misunderstandings. In the following interchange, prompted by a poem about walking by the beach which the class had read, the teacher hears the child's misunderstanding about souls/soles, and although she does not explore the idea of a breathing soul, she does acknowledge it, and then clarifies the kind of sole that is the focus of interest in the poem.

Teacher: What are the soles?
Callum: Where you breathe.
Teacher: We're talking about your feet, Callum. Which part of your foot is the sole of your foot? I know what you mean, you mean the other soul, I think. Which part of

your foot is the sole of your foot? Do you know? [A child holds his foot up.]

Teacher: That's right, hold it up, show us. That bit right at the bottom, isn't it? Sole. So the sand moulds the soles of the feet. Good.

This also ties in with the ideas raised in earlier chapters about effective questioning and high quality classroom interaction, because when teachers used questioning to draw out children's prior knowledge, this allowed them to see where children were coming from. As we have already seen, however, the number of questions eliciting prior knowledge were relatively few. Interviewing children after their lessons showed that children exposed to the same teaching input were deriving different learning outcomes: low achievers were not achieving the same levels of understanding, and were sometimes actively constructing misconceptions, whereas high achievers were making thoughtful and relevant connections and abstracting information (Table 5.3).

In the interviews children often articulated misconceptions which potentially could have been expressed in class. Following the Year 2 science lesson looking at seeds, Sally shows on several occasions that she is thinking of a seed as an egg; she bemoans the fact

Table 5.3 How understanding and misunderstanding relates to gender and ability

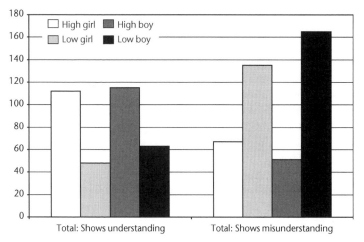

that another child's broad bean seed is growing better than hers because hers is 'still in the egg' and she explains to the interviewer that 'Flowers have [seeds] inside, and they have their eggs, and their little babies.' The connection Sally has made between an egg and a seed is both plausible and logical, and a good building-block for establishing the similarities of seeds and eggs (both the starting points for life) and the differences (seeds develop into plants; eggs develop into animals, including human babies).

Asking questions that invite children to explore their prior knowledge of a topic can make a powerful base for building and developing thinking, and gives the teacher an insight into children's schemata or mental maps for the learning to be addressed. The concept of the schema was discussed in Chapter 1, but it is worth thinking about the practical implications of Nutbrown's comment that 'consideration of children's schemas and children's particular "threads" of thought can be a way of linking theory about how children learn with day-to-day practice' (1994: 123). A few minutes' talk time devoted to eliciting prior knowledge is a practical way to begin to scaffold children's learning effectively, but also to share and construct meaning and understanding together. At the start of a sequence of Year 3 history lessons on the Ancient Egyptians, the teacher asks the class 'Who knows anything about the Ancient Egyptians?', which stimulates a wide-ranging discussion of what they know. One strand of this discussion relates to Egyptian mummies, initiated by one child's comment that 'There's a mummy'. The teacher lets the discussion run, using questions to continue to probe their understanding of mummies. Through this discussion, stimulated by the first child's statement, but sustained by the teacher's questioning, the children reveal a complex picture of truths, half-truths and misconceptions about mummies.

Jack: There's a mummy.
Teacher: Well, I'm a mummy.
Jack: Uh, no.
Teacher: What do you mean by a mummy, Tania?
Tania: It's wrapped up.
Sally: Something wrapped up.
Teacher: Like a Christmas present?
Lou: A person wrapped up in tissue paper.
　　　　[Brief interchange about pharaohs. Charlie puts up hand.]
Teacher: Charlie?
Charlie: They have coffins to put the mummies in.

Tom: I can answer Tania's question?

Teacher: Yes, Tania's question. What she said about mummies; what were you going to say about it?

Tom: The people get killed and they get wrapped up and put in a coffin.

Teacher: Do they get killed or do they just die?

Tom: They get killed.

Teacher: They get killed. Oh right. So you think that people get killed and wrapped up?

Jack: People were getting killed and wrapped up.

Teacher: People were getting killed and wrapped up.

[Further interchanges about coffins]

Luke: Inside them you sometimes get some mummies.

Teacher: Inside?

Joe: The coffins, you get mummies.

Teacher: Inside the coffins you sometimes get mummies, right.

Kylie: They put them inside the wall; they stone them up.

Teacher: They stone them up. What do you mean by stone them up?

Kylie: They put the stone in the wall and they put the stone in the way, carved into the wall.

Teacher: Right, well, they seal them in. Why do they do that?

Sally: So they can't get out.

Teacher: Why would you cover up the wall, so they can't get in there? Joe, have you got any thoughts on that? [Joe puts up his hand]

Teacher: Yes?

Joe: Because the mummies might break out.

Teacher: The mummies might break out! So what's inside the mummy then?

Charlie: A person!

Tracey: A pharaoh!

Teacher: It's a pharaoh or a person, but I'm getting confused here. Are those people dead?

Luke: Yeah! but they're wrapped up . . .

Teacher: Yeah, so how would they get up and come out then? [Lots of talk]

Sally: Someone might break in and open the box.

Teacher: Break in the box?

Jack: Break in bits of the wall.

Teacher: I think we're a little bit confused here. [Lots of answers from the children]

Teacher: Shh!

Naomi: They're real people alive, but there's these people who put them in coffins wrapped up and put them in the wall of the stone and they don't eat anything and they die.

Teacher: Do you think that's what really happens?

Jack: Yes.

From this conversation, the teacher can build a subtle picture of the children's collective understanding about Egyptian mummies and the mummification processes. The interaction can be represented as a schema, mapping strands and ideas elicited during the conversation, as is shown in Figure 5.1.

The schema suggests that children can make the distinction between Egyptian mummies and mothers; that they are aware of some of the mummification processes such as wrapping the body, and sealing tombs with stones; and that they understand some association between mummies and pharoahs. The dialogue also shows some misconceptions too. First, some of the children think people were killed before being made into mummies, rather than it being a burial ritual; second, some of them think the mummies were buried alive; third, some of them think that mummies could come back to life and

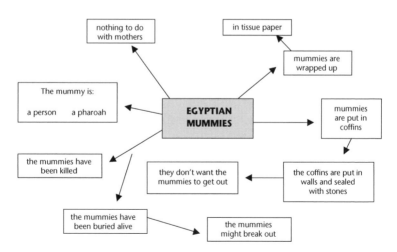

Figure 5.1 A diagram of a schema for 'Egyptian mummies'

break out of the tombs; and fourth, some of the children think the tombs were sealed up to stop the mummies from getting out. The children do not refer to the sources of these misconceptions but they may well come from horror narratives, including children's cartoons and television programmes, where mummies are represented as monsters coming back to life and terrorizing people. So the class schema for 'Egyptian mummies' provides a clear framework and starting-point for developing children's learning.

 Spotlight on Good Practice

- **Devise ways to explore children's schemata.**

    - In pairs, children draw mind maps of what they know about a topic.
    - Collectively on a whiteboard or overhead transparency, elicit children's thinking about a new topic or concept.
    - Use listening triads (two children talking; third child listening and reporting back) to explore prior knowledge.
    - Try asking small groups to come up with a number of facts they know about already in a minute or two at the start of the lesson.

- **Develop questioning strategies that draw on prior knowledge.**

    - Use speculative and open-ended questions that reveal to you how children are thinking.
    - Avoid too many factual recall questions that allow only one response.
    - Use reflective questions to invite children to explore and express their understanding.

- **Use classroom interaction to listen as well as to speak.**

    - Listen carefully to children's responses so that you can pick up on how they are drawing on their prior knowledge.
    - Listen especially to low achievers, and boys, in case they are attempting to use their own experience to engage with school learning.

- **Support children in making connections in their learning.**

  - Invite children to make connections by asking directly about any links they can see between learning addressed in the lesson and anything they have encountered elsewhere, including out of school.
  - Identify the key themes/principles of your lessons. Give the children the key themes in child-speak and ask them in groups to think of ways these themes might be connected. This will draw on prior knowledge and help the children to make connections.
  - Use visual strategies to explore connections and inter-relationships in learning: flowcharts, building blocks, concept maps, arrows.
  - Encourage children to use phrases like 'This reminds me of . . .'; 'We did something like this when . . .'; 'This is like . . .' to help them actively make connections.
  - When planning, consider whether there are prior experiences or prior knowledge from out of school which might help children see links with work being undertaken in school.
  - Be prepared to be flexible about your learning objective so that you can take different paths to the intended goal, including paths initiated by children's responses.

Conclusion

Acknowledging and integrating children's prior knowledge into whole class teaching is a highly challenging and complex endeavour, not least because each child's prior knowledge is unique. Whole class talk is frequently strongly directed towards curriculum goals, framed by sharply focused learning objectives. This does make whole class talk purposeful, but it can mean that interactions are more concerned with confirming understanding, soliciting 'right' answers, and tightly controlling what knowledge is seen as appropriate. Purposeful talk, addressing curriculum goals, does not have to be incompatible with more free-ranging, exploratory talk which balances the imperatives of learning with the imperatives of teaching. Whole class interactions could usefully target eliciting and tackling misconceptions, making explicit attempts to integrate new knowledge with existing knowledge, and trying to perceive the conceptual connections that children are constructing. The metaphor of the teacher as the expert guide is apt, as the teacher's role through classroom interaction is to guide learners along routes and pathways which identify what is known and integrate this with the new.

6 Critical moments in classroom talk

The premise upon which interactive whole class teaching is built is that teacher talk supports children's learning through questions asked and information shared, thus developing the child's understanding through carefully scaffolded interactions. But the relevance of the concept of 'scaffolding' as a metaphor to describe how teachers support the learning of children is dependent upon the awareness that at some point the scaffold will be removed. Previous researchers (Mercer 1995) have argued that too often the scaffold is never removed and this fosters dependence rather than independence amongst children. Through a strong desire to support children, teachers may scaffold learning in such a way that while it may be both safe and strong, it is rather less inclined to give access to new ideas through speculation and reflection, or to lead children towards independent learning. For scaffolding and classroom talk to be effective, the eventual handover to independence has to be anticipated and planned for. Part of the skill of the teacher however is to recognize and capitalize upon those unplanned-for moments at which the handover to independence might occur. Examining critical moments to investigate how teachers manage the handover to independence was one of the questions at the heart of the TALK project.

With the benefit of video recordings of teaching, we were able to search for critical moments and analyse what was happening in these interactions. These moments highlighted the deft skill involved in exploiting an opportunity for learning, and how easy it is to miss such an opportunity. Teaching is of course a dynamic, fluid and spontaneous enterprise; no matter how carefully a lesson is planned, we can never be fully prepared for what a child might say, or where a child's response might lead us. For most of us, it is precisely this spontaneity that makes teaching so exciting! Video recordings confer the great privilege of hindsight and recall, allowing for the kind of reflective analysis that is impossible when engaged in the live act of teaching (and underline once again the considerable potential of video as a professional development tool).

Defining critical moments

So what is a critical moment? Goodwin (2001: 11) refers to critical turning points 'where the teacher's utterances influence the shape and tone of the subsequent interaction'. The TALK project defined a critical moment as a moment in which a teacher's utterance was significant either in the way a child's understanding was developed or in the way it was confounded. Each critical moment is a moment of choice, though in the dynamic reality of the classroom some of these critical moments were missed or misunderstood. In hindsight, the teachers were conscious of the alternative courses they could have pursued: what they should have said or what they wished they had said. We examine this collection of critical moments in the spirit of celebration for what all teachers can do, but tempered with the spirit of realism. Teaching is not a perfect science, but spotlighting real examples of teachers talking to children in their best and worst moments might scaffold our own learning as classroom practitioners.

Asking questions and increasing opportunities for interactivity is always a risky business. A child's answer might miss your point and introduce material that does not form part of your carefully planned lesson. An answer might reveal a misconception, meaning you have to decide whether to pursue new material as planned, or revisit old material. An answer might present opportunities for thinking that you had not anticipated but are well worth pursuing in the lesson. An answer might interest you but you are aware of the forthcoming Key Stage 2 tests, and this answer directs attention away from learning that will help children succeed in the test. Children's answers will definitely reveal that they not only respond at different levels according to their ability, interest or past experience, but may well interpret the question in a variety of different ways. The complexities of interactive teaching are enormous, and for every utterance a child makes, you have to make a virtually split-second decision about how to handle it. One option is to accept the answer and move on quickly, or to quietly ignore the awkward answer.

Take the Year 2 teacher doing a lesson on sharing. The lesson is highly interactive. Everyone is involved and children are given objects to share out between different numbers of friends. The concept being explored is division, and the focus is sharing equally. By ensuring that they start with the right number, and have the right number of friends, the teacher guarantees there will be no problem with numbers that don't share equally as whole numbers, avoiding the tricky problem of working with fractions with Year 2 children. If problems arise, the simple expedient of asking 'Will they share equally?' gives children the straightforward option of saying 'Yes' or 'No'. So when 9 fails to share between 2, the teacher asks the obvious question: 'Can we share 9 equally into 2?' Unfortunately she doesn't receive the anticipated answer.

Charlie knows about sharing and has probably solved some real life sharing problems in practical ways. He replies, 'No . . . we could chop the spare one in half'.

This lesson is about sharing, not fractions, and the teacher does not want to think about halves, but about whole numbers, so she redirects their thinking back to whole numbers and offers an alternative solution: 'We could, but if we keep to whole numbers . . . how about if we give them one more?'

Teachers face complex decisions like this all day. Should you run with the new idea of halving and risk confusing less able children, or stick to the plan? Is this a missed opportunity, or a teacher keeping the lesson clearly focused? Familiar moments such as this one recall Barnes *et al.*'s (1986) critique that talk is used as a tool for teaching, rather than a tool for learning. In practice, it is likely that at different points in the lesson teachers will give different priorities to the teaching needs and the learning needs, attempting to keep some kind of balance between the two. Part of the skill of teaching, and the difficulty, is exercising this judgement.

The critical moments captured on the video recordings underline the complexity of these judgements, and the analysis categorized critical moments into three types, which we discuss in the following sections.

Stick to your plans:
These were critical moments which carefully steered the talk along a predetermined path by:

- eliciting responses from children which were then either ignored or dismissed;

- controlling interaction by strongly cueing the children to a predetermined answer;
- redirecting children's responses to the teacher's agenda.

A bit of a muddle:
These were critical moments which created confusion in learning because of:

- the teacher's insecurity with her own subject knowledge.

Go with the flow:
These were critical moments which were responsive to children's learning by:

- the teacher responding flexibly to the children's responses;
- the teacher creating more opportunity for children to interact with each other and become involved.

Stick to your plans

A significant number of critical moments highlighted the frequency with which the teaching objective took precedence over children's learning experiences. At critical points in lessons, teachers chose to pursue their own agenda rather than recognizing or attending to learners' needs. There were several examples of the teacher not listening to the children's answers, and what these answers were telling them about the child's level of understanding, both in terms of what they misunderstood or what they knew already. There were also examples of the teacher shaping and interpreting children's comments to conform to the teaching objective.

In a Year 2 science lesson, the teacher was exploring the best surface for rolling toy cars along. As a learning objective she had the scientific concept of a fair test in her mind, but knowing that the children in Year 2 have varying capacities to measure accurately, she had predetermined that it would be 'more fair' to use string or multilink bricks.

Teacher: What can we use to measure distance?
Children: [Many suggest a ruler.]

A ruler seemed obvious, and drew on previous experience, but this teacher was going to use string so she probed.

Teacher: Anything else?

Joe: [Picks up a ruler and demonstrates how to use the ruler to measure.]

But this teacher wants to show how string can be used so redirects Joe's answer: 'That wasn't fair because you didn't measure very well. It wouldn't be a fair test then.'

After a few more answers from the children, none of which suggested string, she revealed that she had string in her hand and said, 'What I could use is some string. Put the string from the end of the slope to where the car has gone to. And then I can see that the car travelled this far, this length of string.' The lesson then continues as planned. The critical moment is interesting because the opening question appears speculative, inviting children to solve a problem, but it is in fact a closed question with only one permissible answer – string. At the end of the sequence, you might wonder what the children now think about rulers and how this matches with other life experiences. In what context would string be seen as more accurate than a ruler?

In contrast in the following example, the teacher creates space to acknowledge a child's response. This Year 6 class were considering how to halve the remaining odd penny between two restaurant diners sharing a bill of £46.25. One child drew on his own social knowledge of restaurant behaviour and resolved the mathematical dilemma with a perfectly logical, context related solution:

Teacher: So you have £23 and then you'd have 12 and a half pence.

Jake: You could give them a penny tip, so you could part it equally.

Teacher: Give them a penny tip, you're so generous.

The teacher simply accepts the child's response and gives it credence by repetition and the quip about generosity, then continues with the lesson on halving. The response takes seconds, but demonstrates the kind of on the spot flexibility which can still be compatible with focused teaching.

A similar focus on leading children to a predetermined answer is evident in the following extract from a Year 2 literacy lesson looking at the use of simile in poetry writing. The teacher was so focused upon the answer she wanted to get, that she misses the children's different interpretation of 'light'. Her closed questioning is reinforced by non-verbal signals directing the children to her way of thinking.

Teacher: What is snow lighter than? Snow's falling through the sky very lightly. What does it make you think of? [Indicates with her hands that she means weight.]

Sarah: Stars.

Teacher: Stars? Would stars be light? What made you think of stars? Interesting, any others? 'As light as –'?

Alex: Sun.

Teacher: Oh so you're thinking of light too. What do you think I mean when I say lighter than here? [Again uses balancing action with hands.] What do you think I mean?

Carl: Weight.

Teacher: I was imagining the weight of the snow. What could be lighter than snow?

Lee: The calendar? [There was a calendar on the wall behind the teacher's head.]

Lee's answer is clearly one of confused desperation – he is not grasping the line of questioning and is trying out random answers. The teacher initially missed the connections the children were making between the whiteness of snowflakes and stars, and the double meaning of the word 'light'. Her question 'What made you think of stars?' was a good one at this juncture and would have altered the nature of this critical moment had she allowed the children to explain their thinking. As a consequence, they might have created an unanticipated cluster of similes on brightness, which would still have fulfilled the learning focus of this interaction.

The tendency for teachers to pursue their teaching agenda and consequently not to hear children attempting to give voice to their developing understanding is further illustrated by this example from a lesson on the active and passive voice. The children were shown a picture and two sentences that describe the picture with different subjects: 'The mouse is frightening the elephant' and 'The elephant is being frightened by the mouse'. The purpose of this was to show how the active and passive voice can describe the same event, but with different emphasis. A child, providing a rare example of a question from a child rather than from a teacher, attempted to clarify her understanding of the passive voice, but the teacher's answer shifts from considering the passive, to confirming that adding a relative clause can make a simple sentence into a complex sentence:

Georgie: If you said in the second one that the elephant was frightened by the mouse who was like making faces or something, then would it be like the same thing with the first one?
Teacher: Yes, you would just turn it into a complex sentence.

It is not entirely clear what Georgie is asking, but it does not appear to be primarily concerned with complex sentences, but with some form of comparison between the first and second examples. The teacher did not answer the question the child was asking, however, but instead turned it into a different question, one about complex sentences, the focus of a previous lesson. This was a missed opportunity to find out the level of the child's understanding of the passive and possibly to clarify a confusion or to support and hand over to independence. The opportunity was missed because the teacher's eye was upon curriculum objectives and delivery, not the intellectual demands of learning a complex idea such as the active and passive voice.

Critical moments like these, which are strongly driven by the teacher's agenda, tended to close down thinking and meaningful interactions in favour of playing a guessing game. Children struggled to read the teacher's mind and produced the answers they believed the teacher wanted: a game of hunting for 'right answers', rather than 'reasoned answers'. Occasionally the game is cut short as the teacher answers her own question: 'Does anyone know a word that you use for when a seed has begun to grow? It's a funny word called germinate.' The teacher reflections on these critical moments draw attention to a dilemma, a tension between the need for their teaching to be focused and purposeful with clear objectives for learning, and a considerable amount of curriculum content to be covered with their expressed wish to be responsive to individual children's questions and needs, and a desire to be more flexible with their interactions. In particular, awareness of accountability mechanisms, such as Ofsted, league tables and test data, were seen as strong contributing factors to critical moments that followed the teacher's path, not that of the children.

Box 6.1   Talking point

- How do we balance focused, purposeful teaching with responsive, thoughtful learning?
- How can you resolve the conflict between needing to cover curriculum objectives and needing to meet children's learning needs?

A bit of a muddle

The Primary National Strategy, particularly the Literacy Strategy, expects a high level of subject knowledge, and in some cases such as grammar, requires teachers to teach topics and terminology which they themselves were never taught. One cluster of critical moments revolved around subject knowledge difficulties, including the expression of place value in numeracy, and the concept of the fair test in science. In these critical moments the teacher was struggling with her own subject knowledge, resulting in her unwittingly misleading children. Most examples of critical moments relating to a subject knowledge weakness related to the teaching of grammar. The Year 6 lesson on the passive and active voice, which has already been highlighted, provides another example of a teacher whose own knowledge of this grammatical convention was insecure (Myhill 2003). The post-lesson interviews with the four focus children indicated that they had learned the terms *active* and *passive* but had no real understanding of their function in a sentence. Instead they had developed various misconceptions, including the notion that using passive verbs 'helps add a little bit of interest' to writing, and major confusions about how the active and passive represent agency differently: 'an active verb is to tell you that that person actually made a movement and did that particular thing himself whereas with passive you would say that he did it rather than putting it into how he did do it.'

In another example, a teacher perpetuated a common misconception that adjectives are always ornamental, decorative words and failed to note that in the text being studied, 'existing' is indeed an adjective. Asked what it is that makes an application for planning permission sound formal, a child responded:

Sally:	They don't use very many adjectives and they don't describe the swimming pool.
Teacher:	Right, it's not describing. Perhaps in a story, can anybody think how the swimming pool might be described? Here it just says 'existing swimming pool'. In a story how might you describe the swimming pool? Think of some adjectives to describe a swimming pool.
Jack:	Um, wet.
Teacher:	Yes
Lydia:	Describe how big it was.
Teacher:	Yes, you could describe how big it was, but I think perhaps it could be more expressive, couldn't it, more descriptive. Can you think of some more adjectives you could use to describe a swimming pool?
Molly:	Blue, wet.
Teacher:	Blue and wet.
Luke:	Sparkling.

In trying to help children recognize the difference in language between a planning application and a story, she sets up a misconception about description and the role of adjectives in this. She suggests that formal writing isn't descriptive and therefore needs no adjectives. In the text, the swimming pool *is* described: what is salient is that the planning application uses adjectives to specify and to be precise. It is the nature and purpose of the description and how adjectives are used that discriminate between formal language and a story.

A weakness or gap in subject knowledge does not always have to be a cause of muddle or confusion, and can instead be used to create a classroom climate of shared learning. Children can bring to the classroom relevant experiences, such that they can be the expert, as demonstrated in a Year 6 RE lesson on Islam, when one child in the class came from a Muslim family. The children wanted to know what the imam said from the top of the minaret and the teacher admitted she didn't know. Given the children's interest and insistence that she should find out – 'You should tell us a bit more about that, Miss' – the teacher appealed to the child from a Muslim family to see if he could find the answer for them from his parents. The teacher's response demonstrated her willingness to step down from the role of expert, to go beyond the agenda she had intended to pursue to address the children's agenda, and to use positively the diversity of home experiences present within her class.

Primary school teachers, of course, are in an invidious position of being required to deliver the entire curriculum, regardless of personal strengths and weaknesses. Perhaps the strongest message from this subset of critical moments is that policy initiatives need to be accompanied by constructive professional development which addresses teachers' learning needs, as well as children's learning.

Box 6.2 Talking point

- What interaction strategies will increase sequences of children's responses rather than the conventional teacher–child–teacher turn taking pattern?
- How often do you think you are prepared to go with the flow in your talk interactions?

Go with the flow

The positive examples of teacher interaction in the two previous sections are both examples of a time where the teacher was prepared go with the flow of children's responses and react to what their responses indicated about their learning. There was a whole set of critical moments which exemplified this willingness to go with flow: those turning-point moments in lessons where the teacher decides to leave the planned lesson and follow the children's lead. In these moments teachers show flexibility; they think on their feet because something the child has said is recognized as an opportunity to move thinking forward, or maximize the impact of an idea. Amongst the videoed lessons there are moments when the teacher created space for children to think and opportunities for them to air their thoughts. Sometimes teachers become part of the discussion rather than controllers of it. The following extract comes from a Year 6 numeracy lesson on calculating and using averages. The sequence is initiated by one of the rare moments when a child asked an unsolicited question, which the teacher took as an opportunity to enhance understanding of the key concept 'average'. The teacher recognized the fact that the child was attempting to place the word 'average' in an everyday context in order to explore its meaning. She attempted to scaffold the group's understanding by developing the same strategy, to make connections between the mathematical concept of 'average' and their life experience of the word used in different contexts.

Mark:	Doesn't average mean normal, though?
Teacher:	Have you heard average used anywhere else?
Susie:	Normal, if you are an average person.
Teacher:	Right, you are of average ability you might have heard, yes? By that I mean that there are some people more, some people less, but generally you are in the middle. What about in sport, have you heard it used? In cricket sometimes you hear it used.
David:	The average score that you get.
Teacher:	Average score, batting average, yes? So this is the person with the batting average which means that generally over that game you've got so many runs per over, sometimes you've got less, sometimes you've got more, but if you even it all out this is what you get each over.
Emma:	Average speed.

In other critical moments, the teacher's response changed the typical interaction pattern by disrupting the common teacher–child–teacher–child pattern. There were several examples of teachers deliberately suspending the 'hands up' approach and creating different patterns of interaction to accommodate a particular response. In a Year 6 literacy lesson on argument writing, the teacher realized that her introduction to the topic of capital punishment had provoked strong views and so she gave the children time out to talk to each other about their views before continuing. The teacher reflection recorded by this teacher following this lesson revealed that this was a spontaneous reaction on her part, driven by the children's response rather than a planned event. This intuitive reaction was highly motivating for these children and the rest of the lesson demonstrated high levels of participation and interaction, the children having had the opportunity to rehearse their ideas, and think out loud in a context where their developing opinions were not being aired publicly.

These moments are hard to record in a written text because the interaction is more like real conversation and no longer has the normal turn-taking characteristics. What is noticeable is how many of these examples come from numeracy lessons. In one lesson on shape the teacher invited the class to tell her everything they knew about finding the area of two-dimensional shapes to see if they could use what they knew about these shapes to work out the surface area of three-dimensional shapes. In some respects, the talk here was very chaotic, although the teacher kept control by paraphrasing their contributions and then prompting further thinking. In this way it was the children's thinking that was being used and developed to speculate about possible strategies to solve a problem. The buzz of involvement in this opening few minutes of the lesson set the tone for the rest of the lesson. Similarly the two extracts below, which both come from the same teacher, demonstrate a more conversational style, a style that encouraged the children to think out loud. This teacher allowed conversations between children to run, rather than controlling them by intervening, thus breaking down the traditional turn-taking pattern.

Episode 1

Matt:	Well I was going to say what happens if it's, um, 23.1, how are you going to halve the point one?
Teacher:	Well, it's point one isn't it? So what is point one?
Kate:	One tenth.
Teacher:	One tenth. So what's half of a tenth?
Kylie:	Two.
Clare:	A fifth.
Josh:	0.51 tenths.
Teacher:	Well, what you've brought us to, Josh, actually is . . . a link between decimals and fractions.

Episode 2

Teacher:	What if the bill is 46 pounds, 25 pence, what is the bill each?
Carly:	23 pounds, 12 point 5.
Teacher:	But if I said 23 pounds, 12 points 5, does that look right?
Carly:	No.
Max:	Can I say 23 pounds, 12 pence remainder 1?
Luke:	Remainder 2, actually.
Teacher:	Well you're sat in the restaurant, how are you going to halve the cost?
John:	Well you could split it up, take the 1 from the 5 and then halve the 4 and then you'd have 2p and then see who would pay the odd 1p.

In these lessons there were many more examples of children asking questions, and taking the initiative in terms of how they solve problems. From the teacher's point of view it was quite a risky strategy because she was often led to tackle challenging mathematical ideas, and in some instances there were examples of her thinking aloud just as the children think aloud as she struggled to resolve problems herself. In one lesson she managed to confuse herself as she worked through tricky examples, but because she had the children with her, they pointed out her mistake and helped her realize where she had gone wrong.

> *Charlie:* I was going to say, if you've got that how is it going to lead on to the next one?
>
> *Teacher:* Yes, you're absolutely right. I think I've done it wrong here.
>
> *Lee:* Because you don't know that you're going to have double 228.
>
> *Helen:* So you do half of the next one along. Double the half.
>
> *Teacher:* I think I've done it wrong, yes, I've confused you haven't I? I've confused myself. Sorry kids.

Arguably, this teacher modelled a process of mathematical thinking, but not one based on the omnipotent teacher who always knows the answers, but one who works towards solutions with the children, even if together they have to negotiate wrong turnings.

 ### *Spotlight on Good Practice*

- **Develop your listening skills as a teacher.**

  - Avoid hearing only the answers you anticipated.
  - Listen for the underlying logic or misunderstanding in a child's response not just the surface answer.
  - Develop a habit of hearing yourself as you give responses and reflecting on their helpfulness as you teach.
  - Consider taping or videoing just a 10-minute episode of whole class talk and listen to it just to examine how well you listen to children's responses and how your responses build their learning.

- Pair up with another teacher who is interested in this and in one week consciously think about critical moments and discuss them with each other subsequently. If possible, you could consider observing each other briefly to provide another perspective on critical moments.

- **Develop a repertoire of strategies to manage critical moments.**

  - If a child spontaneously raises a good question, instead of answering it yourself, use a *questioning stick* (a can with a card question mark symbol attached to the top) to indicate that you want the children to answer this question.

  - If a child's response reveals a misconception or misunderstanding, use it as a collective opportunity to think it through. Signal that everyone needs to think by some strategy, such as your putting on a *thinking cap*, and repeat the child's statement. Ask all the class to think about how to respond to the child's statement.

  - Use a critical moment to indicate that you as teacher are not going to respond first but want a series of responses from the class. Take the issue raised by the critical moment (a question, a misunderstanding, a thought) and give the class one minute to discuss it in pairs. Then run a pacy *buzz session* where you take as many answers as possible from the class. During this buzz session, do not comment at all on the responses, simply hear and accept them all, then offer a response at the end if necessary. You could signal that at these moments you are not going to speak by miming that you are zipping up your lips.

  - Use a *think aloud* strategy to share and explore an individual child's thinking. When a critical moment arises, instead of giving a response, invite the child who triggered the critical moment to think aloud, and explain how they came to make that response. This could be followed by asking other children to think aloud as well. Again it might be helpful to signal the think aloud time by having some form of visual indicator, such as a large cardboard think bubble.

- When a child makes a response which is divergent, humorous, quirky or practical, be prepared to acknowledge it, even if you then continue along your intended path of discussion.

- **Make connections.**

  - Many of the strategies for coping creatively and sensitively with critical moments relate to the topics of other chapters, and the spotlights on good practice relating to interactive teaching, questioning, and using prior knowledge are all relevant to managing critical moments.

Conclusion: planning spontaneous moments!

Most of the episodes described in this chapter record moments in classrooms that generally pass unnoticed. The best of these critical moments reveal teachers temporarily relinquishing control of the talk to encourage more child–child interaction and speculative thinking. In these critical moments, teachers scaffold learning by listening sensitively to children's responses, and by generating interactions that are more concerned with process and understanding than with product and knowledge. They represent an alternative scaffolding strategy to the tightly controlled teacher-led interaction which characterized many teaching episodes, and which the teachers themselves, commenting in their post hoc reflections, recognized (Box 6.3).

Box 6.3   Teachers' voices

- My talk is very structured and doesn't allow for the children to develop their individual understanding/ideas.
- How *do* you get the right balance of teacher modelling and pupil/teacher discussion?
- Children need more time to articulate their thoughts and comments.

What is true of all of these critical moments is that they were identified retrospectively: the research team commenting through analysis, the teachers commenting through reflection. Each of these moments is an on-the-spot, live response to a unique situation – which then begs the question: is it possible to plan for such moments? Is it possible to be prepared for the spontaneous, flexible response? Clearly, it is not possible to follow up every utterance a child makes, or pursue every tangential route suggested. The stakeholders in the TALK project were agreed, however, that children's comments are too lightly ignored, too readily shaped and too consistently underused. Black *et al.* (2002: 7) emphasize that children's 'learning may depend less on the capacity to spot the right answer and more on their readiness to express and discuss their own understanding'. The capacity to recognize a critical moment as it occurs, and to seize it as an opportunity for shared learning and thinking, is one well worth developing.

7 Changing classroom practice

At a period in British educational history when there have been more national and political interventions to change classroom practice than perhaps at any other time in history, this chapter considers the role of the teacher in effecting changes in classroom practice. Thus the focus of this chapter alters the lens through which we are considering talking, listening and learning from a child-centred lens to a teacher-centred lens. Teachers are powerful agents of change but also of course powerful preservers of the status quo. You might think about your own responses to national or local initiatives, and whether your reaction has been one of enthusiastic development of your own classroom practice, or angry professional resistance to the proposed changes. For most of us, when suggested changes chime with our own understanding of what is happening in the classroom and address an issue that we feel is real and genuine, we are more motivated to change than when the changes appear to be at best irrelevant, and at worst misguided in our professional judgement of what children need.

One strength of the research model adopted for the TALK project was that it developed from teachers' own professional interests, from a genuine desire to change and improve classroom practice from within. The central focus on how teachers use whole class talk to scaffold children's learning was not selected because of the university's research team's interest in this area but because the INSET day had stimulated an awareness of potential problems in this area. This sense of ownership was important, as Helen articulated at the end of the project: 'I liked it that it was school generated and not imposed. Our question was chosen by ourselves, so that its application benefited the areas of teaching we wished to improve, because of our own evaluation.' This book has emphasized the importance and significance of the teachers' participation at all levels, not simply as subjects of research, but as active researchers, as agents of research. Taber reminds us that schools are not simply 'data collection sites' for 'outsiders' (2002: 436) and it is a significant feature of the TALK project that the process of being actively involved in the project gave teachers an impetus to change their own practice, both through discussing, critiquing and reflecting on the research findings, and by developing practical strategies to trial in their own classrooms which might improve the benefits to children of teacher talk. The teachers' voices, capturing their thoughts and reflections, form an integral part of this chapter, revealing how they worked towards changing their classroom practice through the research; and how teaching strategies were developed and changed as a result of the project. They also express what still remains to be developed; and from their experiences come suggestions for stimulating reflection on practice which can be used in a school context.

Development of professional thinking through reflective practice

The understanding that professional practitioners can be instrumental in improving their own practice through reflection on practice has long been recognized (Schön 1990). It is a notion that underpins development of practice in both teaching and medicine and is currently receiving wider application nationally as mentoring and coaching become established methods of improving practice in many walks of life. It is axiomatic that the most powerful changes occur because practitioners recognize a need for change. Indeed, schools are now embracing the idea of mentoring and coaching as a means of improving children's progress and learning. This process is based on structured thinking and dialogue focused on specific aspects of practice and leading to the development of new practice from detailed examination of existing routines. Central to Schön's notion of reflective practice is that we look backwards in order to move forwards: by reflecting on our teaching experiences, thinking through their implications, and developing new ways of working that address issues raised, we change our own practice. Moreover, it is a reflective cycle that continues – new ways of working themselves become the source of reflection and re-evaluation.

While Schön tends to see the teacher as a lone practitioner, working on his or her own to improve practice, more recent thinking about how we learn as professionals has placed much more emphasis upon learning together, and the social nature of learning. Lave and Wenger (1991) propose that professional learning occurs within 'communities of practice', with shared values, goals and contexts which can draw on theoretical perspectives and consider them in applied professional settings. In this sense, improving classroom practice is 'situated learning', where there is a common purpose for investigation, grounded in a shared context and understanding.

Although the idea of reflective practice is well-established as a potentially effective means of changing classroom practice, teachers rarely have the opportunity to implement this coherently within an institution. Buchmann and Floden (1993) note that the process of reflection requires supportive structures if effective critical reflection is to occur. Often this may be a framework, real or conceptual, to guide the reflective process. Such support is vital if the person involved in reflection on practice is to move from technical detail to a more thorough and demanding conceptualization of current routines and the development of new practices that are not based merely in technical considerations but which also take account of theoretical underpinnings. Buchmann and Floden (1993) also note that in order to facilitate this, it is necessary to create time and space for the process of reflection. Chapter 2 has already described the design of the TALK research, including the use of video and the reflective prompts. At this point, it is worth signalling that both the video recording and the reflective prompt sheet were support frameworks for critical reflection. A further feature of the TALK project was that the funding bought quality time for the teachers not only to reflect in privacy on their own teaching, but also to meet together to share thoughts, consider findings, and develop new practices.

In the light of both Schön's thinking about reflective practice and Lave and Wenger's emphasis upon learning together in communities

---

Box 7.1 Talking point

- What opportunities do you have to reflect on your own classroom practice?
- Who decides what aspects of teaching and learning you should be developing?
- How do you and your colleagues structure the thinking process to develop new practices?

of practice, it was important that collaborative learning was a feature of the TALK project from the outset. At an early stage, all the teachers shared the responsibility for reading and disseminating aspects of the background research literature to their colleagues. This established a non-hierarchical framework in which responsibility was shared equally and where all contributions were of equal value. As the project developed, teachers saw benefits in collaborative practice both for themselves and for the school. Planned opportunities for discussion of shared aims and experiences proved beneficial and supportive at several levels. There was a developing sense of collegiality in knowing that each participant could both learn from others but also contribute to shared knowledge, in many senses replicating what was happening in the classroom. The teachers appreciated being able to work collaboratively to improve both individual practice and whole school approaches, and talking and listening were at the heart of the learning that was occurring:

> I enjoyed the intellectual stimulus of discussing teaching methods and children's learning in fine detail with very committed colleagues.
>
> (Sarah)

> Working as a group of classroom practitioners, it has been both stimulating, challenging and reassuring to recognize that there are common factors that impact on our work.
>
> (Marge)

> We ended up drawing upon other colleagues' research to inform our own teaching.
>
> (Helen)

> [It was valuable] sharing practice used by others.
>
> (Lucy)

> The chance to learn from other professionals.
>
> (Laura)

Just as the classroom research has indicated how important it is for children to be active participants in classroom talk, and to be given more opportunities for discussion and exploration of ideas, so the process of professional learning adopted by the TALK project underlines that it is equally important for teachers to enjoy parallel opportunities for genuinely purposeful discussion and shared learning. You might ask whether the pattern of teachers tending to dominate classroom talk identified in this study is mirrored on INSET courses and National Strategy training courses by the domination of PowerPoint and overhead transparencies accompanied by presenter talk. You might also do a quick mental calculation of how much time and opportunity you personally had for discussion, as opposed to listening, and the extent to which your thinking changed. On one level, involvement in professional discussion heightened thinking about the ways in which whole class teacher talk 'impacts on our core purpose of children's learning', and ways of 'making the process of teaching and learning more effective'. More specifically however, dialogue also changed teachers' thinking about 'the teaching and learning in my own classroom', particularly with reference to children's participation and finding 'new ways of involving children in their learning' with 'maximum participation from my class'.

Enabling change in classroom practice

Through the processes of reflection, professional dialogue and changing thinking, the TALK project aimed to identify key issues related to whole class teacher talk and to consider ways to change classroom practice as a consequence. At the outset of the project, the teachers articulated their own beliefs about the importance of talk. Their reflections on the video recording of a series of three of their own teaching episodes allowed the teachers to analyse how the beliefs they had conceptualized at the start of the project were realized in practice. By use of the video evidence and the prompts for reflection they were able to note both difference in children's participation in the lessons but also more subtle and sophisticated teaching patterns which had led to this; they were able to note not only effect but cause as well. They were able to recognize patterns in their own practice which could inhibit effective learning and they were able to conceptualize areas they needed to address – for example, giving structure to the scaffolding of talk episodes, or giving more time for the children to begin to form their ideas – rather than simply focusing on technical aspects or practice. The reflections were detailed and committed, and showed a willingness to accept that attempts to change patterns of teacher and pupil interaction had been both successful in some areas and less successful in others. They were *enabled*, a word which appears several times in their own comments, by the process of participation and reflection to think about changing their classroom practice:

> How many teachers are *enabled* (to have) this opportunity?
>
> (Wendy)

> It has *enabled* me to analyse the impact of different teaching methods I already use.
>
> (Kate)

> The TALK project has *enabled* me to consider the participation levels within my own classroom.
>
> (Barbara)

> Being part of the TALK project has *enabled* me to develop my skills and expertise with using paired work – with Year 1 children.
>
> (Sarah)

> [It has] *enabled* me to raise the profile of talk within the classroom.
>
> (Paula)

> [It has] *enabled* me to help teachers reflect on their practice for the benefit of pupils' learning.
>
> (Denise)

> It has *enabled* me to reflect on my own practice.
>
> (Lucy)

The opportunities for professional discussion and dialogue appear to have been a powerful process for these teachers, enabling the participants to think beyond practices to principles. It is noticeable that the comments made above all address deeper levels of thinking and principles of learning, and there are no references to teaching resources or tips for teaching. The thinking generated through professional talk meant that these teachers generated their own ideas and strategies for the classroom in response to the problems and issues they were identifying. This is a very different kind of 'enabling' than

---

Box 7.2 Talking point

- What enables you to have the confidence to examine and develop your own practice?
- How could your school ensure that there are opportunities for professional dialogue and collaboration as colleagues?

---

might be gained through a folder of practical strategies to take back to the classroom.

Of course, changing thinking of itself does not change classroom practice, though it may be a necessary prerequisite. Allowing teachers to find solutions or possible ways of improving a situation in response to an identified and shared problem is thus a potentially powerful mode of enabling change in classroom practice. At the end of the first year of the study, all the teachers and researchers involved met for a day to discuss the preliminary findings, but more importantly, to design the next stage in the research. From the initial research findings, the teachers identified six interrelated aspects of classroom talk which they felt would benefit from targeted attempts to improve classroom practice. These six areas were:

- generating participation in talk;
- effective questioning;
- effective explanation;
- using prior knowledge;
- listening and responding; and
- making connections.

The teachers then worked together to consider strategies to address each of these areas, and trialled them in their classrooms. They produced a set of guideline materials for each of these six areas which other teachers, not involved with the project, could use. To avoid these simply being a set of 'tips for teachers', they devised a common format for each set of materials, which encouraged other readers to think about the underlying issues and processes, not just the practical strategies. For each identified area first the research findings were summarized, then a selection of teachers' reflections were presented, next *thinking points* were presented to stimulate those using the materials to consider the theoretical underpinning of the TALK strand in the context of their own practice. This led to an example of identi-fied *good practice* from the Phase 1 research, a mini case study. Finally, there was a list of bullet-pointed *things to try in your own classroom*. This structure encouraged metacognition and gave a model of how to move from identified classroom problems to a principled change in classroom practice. It was also a scaffold to encourage any teachers using it to reflect on their own practice at a deeper level. At the con-clusion of the project, the suggested classroom strategies were evalu-ated and amended, and many of these ideas form the foundation for the 'Spotlight on Good Practice' sections in this book.

The appetite stimulated by involvement in this project generated an additional line of classroom-focused collaborative research that had been unanticipated at the outset. Twelve of the participant teachers successfully applied for DfES Best Practice Research Scholar-ships (BPRS), which allowed them to identify a specific focus for their own classroom-based research based on the outcomes of the initial phase of the research. Rather oddly, the BPRS scheme (now discontinued) would not allow joint applications to investigate the same area, which seems to prevent just the kind of collaborative research and shared investigation and thinking that we are advo-cating. However, the collaboration was sustained by building into the BPRS design three research days where all participants gathered to talk and share plans, ideas, research tools and reading. At the final day, each teacher presented the findings of their individual study, but, of course, because all the research questions (see Table 7.1) had their origin in the TALK research, there were many productive interrelationships and considerable topical coherence in the set of studies.

At this juncture, it might be wise to pause and add the caveat that, despite the overwhelmingly positive response of the teachers to involvement in classroom-based research, as recorded above, it would be naive to assume that simply creating opportunities for pro-fessional dialogue and reflection would effect changes in classroom practice. Some changes are easier to implement than others, and some desired changes are influenced by complex sets of interrelating influences, which make change harder to accomplish. In the next two sections of this chapter, we illustrate one example of classroom practice which changed significantly as a consequence of the TALK project, and one which did not change at all, despite explicit efforts to do so.

Table 7.1   The Best Practice Research Scholarship research questions

---

- Does combining kinaesthetic activities with listening activities generate greater participation of Foundation Stage children in whole class interactions?
- Does increasing the opportunities for pair work increase the levels of participation of Year 1 children in whole class teaching?
- Do strategies which avoid the conventional pattern of teacher–pupil–teacher interaction increase the level of participation of children in Year 2 in whole class interaction?
- What can we learn from children's responses in the early years about how they are making connections between their prior knowledge and new learning?
- What teaching strategies enable teachers to make better use of children's prior knowledge?
- What might be appropriate and effective use of process questions in literacy?
- What strategies are successful in involving boys in whole class interactions?
- Can increasing the number of process questions in literacy improve children's thinking about their learning?
- What are the purposes of questions in my whole class teaching?
- What strategies are successful in involving more children in whole class interaction?
- What strategies are successful in involving more children in whole class interaction in numeracy lessons?
- How do teachers' questions enable or disable children from making connections between their prior knowledge and new learning?

Changed patterns of interaction

In the first phase of the study, the most prominent interaction pattern for whole class teaching was the teacher–child–teacher (ping-pong) interaction, where the teacher sat at the front of the class commanding the children's attention throughout the episode (as outlined in Chapter 3). Indeed, there was only one example in the 54 episodes recorded of a teacher deliberately breaking this pattern and encouraging the children to talk in pairs for a minute. In other words, in Phase 1, only one minute of all 54 episodes captured was not whole class teacher–child–teacher–child interaction. Reflecting on this pattern, and the accompanying recognition that this tended to create passive children, some of whom were reluctant to participate, the teachers felt this could be changed to establish more lively and participatory talk scenarios. In effect, they reconceptualized whole class teaching as encompassing a wider set of interactions than the teacher addressing 30 children and taking responses from them in turn. This included trying to encourage child–child interaction where children respond to each other in whole class settings, rather than automatically waiting for the teacher to insert a comment or further question in between every child's answer. It also included other strategies, such as pair work, followed by focused feedback.

When the data from the second phase was analysed, it was evident that there were far more examples of the conventional teacher–child–teacher pattern being disrupted. So, although the traditional 'ping- pong' pattern was still the prevalent pattern, the time engaged in this kind of interaction was far less. In Phase 2, there are 14 examples of teachers deliberately breaking this cycle. Some of these altered patterns are situations where the teacher allows children to answer each other or to make multiple responses to a question. The following extract exemplifies this pattern at its simplest level, where more than one child speaks between teacher utterances:

Teacher: Can you see?
Child: I think it's a pigeon.
Child: I think it's a sparrow.
Teacher: I'm going to tell you what it is in the end. OK. So here's my membership card; here's my scarf.
Children: [various conversations]
Child: It's a little duck.
Teacher: Now, because I'm a member I get lots and lots of letters and again, and can you see this?
Child: Yes.
Teacher: And inside it's got . . .
Child: [inaudible interruption]
Teacher: Lots and lots of things that I have to do 'cos I'm a member, and on all the letters, look, is it the same?
Children: Yeah!
Child: No, it's not the same.
Teacher: I know it's not coloured, but is it the same?

More common, however, were total breaks in the teacher–whole class teaching situation to small bursts of pair work, which for a brief spell had the majority of children engaged in interactions with each other, with the teacher being a less dominant presence. For example, in one Year 1 lesson, children had to use cardboard microphones to interview each other about their families in the middle of a whole class episode exploring belonging and identity. In a Year 2 numeracy lesson, the teacher intersected her introductory section with a paired numeracy activity which gave the children an opportunity to practise the skills she had been introducing before resuming her introduction. Another variation was the use of a physical activity accompanying the whole class talk. In one Year 2 literacy lesson, exploring a poem about walking barefoot on sand, the teacher asked children to stand barefoot in a bowl of sand and describe how it felt, making connections for children between language and experience, and supporting their responses to the poem. The difference between Phase 1 and Phase 2 in the distribution of interactions in whole class teaching is highlighted dramatically by counting the total number of minutes on the video data which exemplify the conventional interaction pattern and the total number of minutes where this pattern is broken in some way. The single instance of a changed pattern in the first phase was when one teacher deliberately altered the teacher–whole class pattern by giving children one minute 'time out' to discuss their responses to capital punishment, a total of one minute out of 54 episodes observed. In contrast, in Phase 2, even though the total length of video recordings made was much shorter overall, the amount of time spent in interactions which were not teacher–whole class was 34 minutes.

So, in Phase 2, after consciously trying to change classroom practice, approximately one-fifth of the time involved children interacting directly with each other, compared with almost 100 per cent teacher–whole class in Phase 1. This represents a significant change in the overall pattern of classroom discourse in whole class teaching and, from the child's perspective, a significant alteration in the nature of engagement in whole class teaching.

Equally important, however, and consistent with Schon's reflective cycle, the changes in classroom practice evident in the second

Table 7.2 Comparison of classroom interaction patterns in Phases 1 and 2

	Phase 1	Phase 2
Teacher–whole class interactions	809 minutes	236 minutes
Alternate patterns, such as pair work, etc.	1 minute	34 minutes

phase were the beginning of a further stage of reflection and development, as the process of watching the interactions closely on video raised further questions. Thus key ideas for further development emerged from individual and shared reflection:

- looking at pairings: should children work with someone they like or should pairings be time or task managed? It was felt important that children get used to working with different partners;
- developing the idea of pairs exchanging views and supporting each other in deciding what further knowledge was needed. The interactions between pairs were found particularly productive;
- providing better time and task structures for group or paired work;
- developing interview activities as a structure work for encouraging talk and finding strategies in supporting the participation of less confident pupils;
- finding ways of working without the need to put hands up which will also encourage the children who contribute less frequently;
- finding ways to extend the opportunity to talk in whole class situations. A way to do this may be to relate to children's prior experiences;
- allowing the children more autonomy and control in the use of talk.

Unchanged classroom practice

If one goal for improvement arising from the first phase was generating greater involvement, participation and engagement in whole class talk settings by disrupting the teacher–child–teacher interaction pattern, a second key goal was to alter the quality of interactions through more effective questioning. However, despite this being an explicit focus for change identified by the teachers and willingly pursued by them, there were almost no significant changes whatsoever between Phases 1 and 2. In fact there was a tiny decrease in the number of speculative and process questions used, and these were the very types of questions the teachers were trying to increase.

Table 7.3 Comparison of types of questions in Phase 1 and Phase 2

Teachers' questions	% Phase 1	% Phase 2
PROCEDURAL	8	12
FACTUAL	64	65
SPECULATIVE	16	15
PROCESS	12	8
	100	100

This suggests that the pattern of teacher discourse may be a heavily embedded professional discourse pattern which is not easily changed, even with the willing and committed engagement of teachers in the process. The fact that changes in the nature of talk did not occur may be because the majority of teacher talk in the classroom is unrehearsed in delivery even when content is planned. We do not plan actual utterances in our class talk, even when we have planned what the content of our talk might be, and most of our teacher talk in the classroom is spontaneous and unrehearsed. It may be that this unrehearsed talk is heavily routinized, and deeply socioculturally determined. It may be easier to generate change using practical strategies which may be planned for, discussed, evaluated, such as greater use of pair work, than it is to fundamentally change the nature of teacher talk itself. However, it is also possible that changes in the way we talk and question in the classroom occur through evolution, rather than revolution, and that the process of change is slower than the time allowed in this research study. Certainly there is evidence of subtle alterations in the discourse patterns, particularly in the qualitative data, and the teacher reflections strongly suggest that they are on a trajectory of development which could be ongoing, if interest and commitment can be sustained.

Conclusion

In the current educational climate there is an increased emphasis on teachers taking responsibility for their own professional development. The notion of the reflective practitioner is not new nor is the idea of a community of learning or practice. It is also clear that given

---

Box 7.3 Teachers' voices

- This has been such a powerful way for teachers to truly evaluate their classroom practice.
- I feel really privileged to have had this opportunity.
- It has really inspired me to reflect on my own practice.
- [It has given me the] opportunity to build in 'flexibility' into my teaching in order to test hypotheses.
- [I've learnt that] nothing can be taken for granted.
- [It has] encouraged me to try something new.

---

time, opportunity and personal relevance, teachers are very willing to play an active part in reassessing old skills and developing new ones to support effective learning in the classroom. However, it is also clear that such processes can be more readily facilitated within the context of a community collaborating and working together for a common learning purpose. This may mean identifying common elements of practice to develop; constructing means of collaborating and co-constructing the developing knowledge about that practice; and providing structures to enable this development. It appears that common elements of success in the TALK project were the sharing of knowledge; a parallel sense of an individual sense of ownership of aspects of the project; and, by no means least, the provision of time and place and the structures for the collaboration and thinking to take place.

Conclusion

The soundbyte or newspaper headline report of this research might well spotlight the ironies of the title of this book: teachers are talking, children are listening, but who is learning? Indeed, the outcomes of the study in their broadest terms do illustrate that the patterns of teacher dominance of classroom talk that have been evident in so many previous studies are still a common feature of our primary classrooms, despite the policy initiatives which have promoted interactive whole class teaching. Unless all the teachers involved in the TALK project are curiously atypical, teachers are talking more than children, they are asking predominantly factual, closed questions, and they make relatively little use of children's prior knowledge, particularly out-of-school knowledge. However, while this may paint the broad brushstrokes of the research, the finer details do show greater subtlety and complexity. The factual, closed questions are sometimes part of careful sequences to build children's thinking, and there are those critical moments when teachers go 'off script' to pursue ideas and thought chains triggered by a child's response. Teachers are very consciously trying to manage children's learning in whole class teaching and to use talk in a manner which is unlike any other context where talk is used. As Alexander (2003: 34) observes, classroom talk appears natural and spontaneous, yet is intrinsically managed and with a clear goal in mind:

> Where conversation is – or purports to be – locally managed, classroom dialogue is teacher managed. Where the end point of conversation may not be clear at the outset, in classroom dialogue, for the teacher at least, it is. Conversation may go nowhere. Equally, it may spectacularly open up the unexpected. Classroom dialogue in contrast steers a safer course. Where conversation may consist of a sequence of unchained two-part exchanges, as participants talk at or past

> each other . . . classroom dialogue explicitly seeks to chain exchanges into a meaningful sequence.

Balancing the demands of management and purposeful direction with talk which is exploratory, responsive and relevant to individual needs is no mean feat. This is compounded when pressures from outside the professional values of the classroom seem to urge contrary practices. The teachers in the TALK project expressed considerable tension between their professional judgement about when to deviate from planned, objective-led routes to address emerging problems or issues related to learning and the regulatory pressure of Ofsted inspection and guidance provided in training for the National Numeracy and Literacy Strategies. The teachers in Hargreaves *et al.*'s study (2002: 2) valued interactive teaching but felt 'it should not get in the way of the pace and objectives of the lesson', a perspective which implies that interactive teaching is about entertainment and fun, but is not actually central to the processes of learning. This does raise questions about whether the training model for introducing teachers to the interactive methods required by the National Literacy and National Numeracy Strategies is an adequate one. It may have focused rather more on the surface features of interactive teaching such as pace, and practical teaching strategies for whole class teaching such as Big Books and number fans, than on the deep structures of talk to scaffold learning and how to develop interactivity that is not simply concerned with involvement and coverage, but with developing shared learning and understanding. There are clear implications for policy here, not least how to achieve a balance between sharply-specified curricula and professional freedom to respond to children's learning needs, but also how to support professional development in appropriate ways.

Talking, listening and learning effectively does require a shift from what are often deeply routinized classroom practices, and which are probably part of our professional self-image as teachers. Arguably, as teachers we are in the classroom because we know the right answers, or perhaps more subtly, because we have access to a particular body of knowledge and understanding, and we have a responsibility to ensure that children acquire this understanding. Culturally, British classrooms are different from those in Europe, as Alexander (2002) has shown, and changing cultural views of the classroom and the role of the teacher cannot be achieved quickly by policy diktat. The emphasis on whole class teaching introduced by the National Strategies for Literacy and Numeracy may have derived from a Far Eastern learning culture, but translated into a British context may have reinforced transmissive teaching, strongly directed towards a 'right' answer. In this scenario, the teacher's question is all-important in securing the 'right' answer, and the child's answer closes the exchange, rather than it being 'the true centre of gravity' (Alexander 2003). The teachers involved in this study demonstrate that change is possible, however, even if change is small and evolutionary, rather than revolutionary. In the short extract below, taken from the second phase of the TALK project, when teachers were exploring how to use talk in a more learning-centred way, the teacher of this Year 2 numeracy lesson does not follow her previous practice of pacy selection of children until the right answer is received, but instead changes her practice in two significant ways. First, she invites other children to help, rather than positioning herself as the sole repository of useful information, and second, she gives the children time to think:

> *Teacher:* No, you were right [talks to the child who has answered]. It is 10, well done . . . ok, and Helena, what do you think this number is?
> *Helena:* 25?
> *Teacher:* Close, but not quite. Who can help her? [Children put their hands up, teacher nods to one to answer.]
> *John:* 35.
> *Teacher:* It's not 35. I'll give you time to think.

This is only the beginning of the story; the ending remains to be written. You could consider what other strategies or questions this teacher could have used to open up this dialogue further. What questions might have illuminated how Helena and John were thinking, and how could the teacher convey that the help she was inviting was less about the right answer, but help in thinking about how to calculate the right answer. How could the teacher step back from her alternating participation in the dialogue? Edwards (2003: 42) maintains that 'the sharpest contrast between whole-class question-and-answer, and whole-class dialogue, is that different and even competing ideas can be kept in play without being subjected to one participant's authoritative arbitration' but relinquishing apparent control is a risky business. However, if classroom learning conversations are to develop into 'coherent and expanding chains of enquiry and understanding', then we need to think about control in a different way, because 'if we want children to talk to learn – as well as learn to talk – then what they say actually matters more than what teachers say' (Alexander 2003: 37).

We invite you to write the end of this story.

Appendix

ANALYSING STATEMENTS: CODING GRID

	Class manage-ment	Establishing group relation-ships	Trans-mission of facts	Trans-mission of strategy	Managing task	Introducing topic or concept	Developing thinking	Affirmation	Recap or summary	Developing vocabulary	Using prior knowledge	Offering guidance or support	Giving reasons for learning	Refocusing	Teacher's agenda	TOTAL
INFORMING																
EXPLAINING																
INSTRUCTING																
SOCIALIZING																
ELABORATING																

DEFINITIONS OF FORMS OF STATEMENTS	
Informing:	Statements which give information about the subject matter and learning purposes
Explaining:	Statements which make connections between ideas, or introduce and explain concepts
Instructing:	Statements which tell the children what to do, either related to behaviour or learning/task
Socializing:	Statements which establish interpersonal relationships within the class
Elaborating:	Statements which take the child's answer and expand, add to or correct it

DEFINITIONS OF FUNCTIONS OF STATEMENTS	
Class management:	Related to the management of behaviour or the management of the lesson
Establishing group relationships:	Conversational comments, throwaway remarks, jokes, comments that rely on the teacher's understanding of the group or of individuals and of shared experiences
Transmission of facts:	Relating knowledge/information
Transmission of strategy:	Explaining how to do something
Managing task:	Managing, sustaining, developing and refocusing a given task
Introducing topic or concept:	Introducing topics or concepts
Developing thinking:	Provoking reflection, speculation, or imagination
Affirmation:	Responding positively to children's input.
Recap and summary:	Either referring to a previous lesson, or to earlier in the lesson, or drawing together the concepts that have been explored in the lesson
Developing vocabulary:	Explaining the meaning of words, or extending vocabulary by including other words that mean the same thing.
Using prior knowledge:	Scaffolding concepts or ideas by building on knowledge that is familiar and understood.
Offering guidance or support:	Usually linked to a task or a question that has been asked and the teacher supports the child by talking through the task, prompting, reminding encouraging, leading the child to the solution or the completion of the task
Giving reasons for learning:	Explaining the rationale of the lesson or why they need to know it
Refocusing:	Bringing the class back to the lesson aims
Teacher's agenda:	Answering own question, rephrasing a child's response, interpreting child's response in terms of lesson aims rather that responding to what has been said

ANALYSING QUESTIONS: CODING-GRID

	Class Manage-ment	Factual elicitation	Cued elicitation	Building on content	Building on thinking	Recapping	Practising skills	Checking prior knowledge	Developing vocabulary	Checking under-standing	Developing reflection on learning	TOTAL
PROCEDURAL												
FACTUAL												
SPECULATIVE												
PROCESS												

Number of pseudo-open or pseudo-speculative questions

DEFINITIONS OF FORMS OF QUESTIONS		DEFINITIONS OF FUNCTIONS OF QUESTIONS	
Factual:	questions which invite a predetermined answer, e.g. *What is 5 plus 5?* *Why do plants have flowers?* *What else could I use to measure?*	Class management: Factual elicitation: Cued elicitation: Practising skills:	related to management of behaviour/tasks asking for recall of fact/information giving clues to answer inviting children to rehearse, repeat or practise a strategy or grasp of understanding e.g. how to divide by two or practising identifying verbs in writing
Speculative:	questions which invite a response with no predetermined answer, often opinions, hypotheses, imaginings, ideas, e.g. *Anyone got any ideas what that could mean?* *Do you think zoos are a good idea?* *Anyone got any opinions about those three children?* *If I made the slope higher, what do you think might happen then?*	Building on content: Building on thinking: Recapping: Checking prior knowledge:	gathering information about the topic/theme making children think about the ideas and concepts; this moves ideas forward, unlike the checking understanding which looks back at ideas already covered recalling past lessons and work done in this lesson checking child's knowledge and experience outside of school which might be relevant to lesson
Procedural:	questions which relate to the organization and management of the lesson, e.g. *Can you all see?*	Developing vocabulary: Checking understanding:	testing/clarifying understanding of words querying understanding and checking grasp of learning undertaken
Process:	questions which invite children to articulate their understanding of learning processes/explain their thinking, e.g. *How did you work that out?* *How do you know that?* *Can you explain why?*	Developing reflection on learning:	inviting children to think about how they are learning and the strategies they are using

References

Alexander, R.J. (2002) *Culture and Pedagogy: International Comparisons in Primary Education*. London: Blackwell.

Alexander, R.J. (2003) Talk in Teaching and Learning: international perspectives in Qualifications and Curriculum Authority, *New Perspectives on Spoken English in the Classroom*. London: QCA.

Alexander, R.J. (2004) *Towards Dialogic Teaching: Rethinking Classroom Talk*. York: Dialogos.

Allerton, M. (1993) Am I asking the right questions? *International Journal of Early Childhood Education*, 25(1): 42–8.

Bakhtin, M. (1981) *The Dialogic Imagination: Four Essays* (edited M. Holquist and trans. C. Emerson and M. Holquist). Austin, TX: University of Texas Press.

Barnes, D. (1976) *From Communication to Curriculum*. Harmondsworth: Penguin.

Barnes, D., Britton, J. and Torbe, M. (1986) *Language, the Learner and the School*, 3rd edn. Harmondworth: Penguin.

Bartlett, F.C. (1932) *Remembering: A Study in Experimental and Social Psychology*. London: Cambridge University Press.

Bennett, S.N., Desforges, C.W., Cockburn, A. and Wilkinson, B. (1984) *The Quality of Pupil Learning Experiences*. London: Lawrence Erlbaum.

Bernstein, B. (1971) *Class, Codes and Control*. London: Routledge and Kegan Paul.

Black, P. and William, D. (1998) *Inside the Black Box: Raising Standards through Classroom Assessment*. London: King's College.

Black, P., Harrison, C., Lee, C., Marshall, B. and William, D. (2002) *Working Inside the Black Box*. London: King's College.

Bousted, M. (1989) Who talks? *English in Education*, 23(1): 41–51.

Britton, J. (1970) *Language and Learning*. London: Penguin.

Bruner, J.S. (1978) The role of dialogue in language acquisition, in A. Sinclair, R. Jarvella and W. Levelt (eds) *The Child's Conception of Language*. New York: Springer-Verlag.

Bruner, J. (1986) *Actual Minds, Possible Worlds*. Cambridge, MA: Harvard University Press.

Buchmann, M. and Floden, R. (1993) *Detachment and Concern – Conversations in the Philosophy of Teaching and Teacher Education*. Cassell: London.

Cook, G. (1989) *Discourse*. Oxford: Oxford University Press.

Cook-Gumperz, J. (1986) *The Social Construction of Literacy*. Cambridge: Cambridge University Press.

Cooper, P. and McIntyre, D. (1994) Patterns of interaction between teachers' and students' classroom thinking and their implications for the provision of learning opportunities, *Teaching and Teacher Education*, 10(6): 633–46.

Corden, R. (2000) *Literacy and Learning through Talk*. Buckingham: Open University Press.

Department for Education (1995) *English in the National Curriculum*. London: HMSO.

Department for Education and Science (1975) *A Language for Life: A Report of the Committee of Inquiry appointed by the Secretary of State for Education and Science under the Chairmanship of Sir Alan Bullock*. London: HMSO.

Department for Education and Science (DES) (1990) *English in the National Curriculum*. London: HMSO.

Department for Education and Employment (DfEE) (1998) *The National Literacy Strategy. A Framework for Teaching*. Sudbury: DfEE.

Department for Education and Employment (DfEE) (1999) *The National Numeracy Strategy. A Framework for Teaching Mathematics from Reception to Year 6*. Sudbury: DfEE.

Department for Education and Employment (DfEE) (2001) *The National Strategy for Key Stage 3: Framework for Teaching English*. London: DfEE.

Department for Education and Skills (DfES) (2002) *Standards for the Award of Qualified Teacher Status*. London: DfES.

Department for Education and Skills (DfES) (2003) *Speaking, Listening, Learning: Working with Children in Key Stages 1 and 2*. London: DfES.

Dillon, J.T. (1988) *Questioning and Teaching*. New York: Teachers' College Press.

Dochy, F. (1992) *Assessment of Prior Knowledge as a Determinant for Future Learning*. Utrecht: Lemma B.V.

Edwards, A.D. and Westgate, D.P.G. (1994) *Investigating Classroom Talk*, 2nd edn. London: Falmer Press.

Edwards, D. and Mercer, N. (1987) *Common Knowledge*. London: Methuen.

Edwards, T. (2003) Purposes and characteristics of whole-class dialogue in

Qualifications and Curriculum Authority, *New Perspectives on Spoken English in the Classroom*. London: QCA.

Foster, P. (1999) 'Never mind the quality, feel the impact': a methodological assessment of teacher research sponsored by the Teacher Training Agency, *British Educational Research Journal*, 47(4): 380–98.

Galton, M., Hargreaves, L., Comber, C., Wall, D. and Pell, A. (1999) Changes in patterns of teacher interaction in primary classrooms: 1976–1996, *British Educational Research Journal*, 25(1): 23–37.

Goodwin, P. (ed) (2001) *The Articulate Classroom*. London: David Fulton.

Gorard, S. (2002) Political control: a way forward for educational research? *British Educational Research Journal*, 50(3): 378–89.

Hargreaves, L., Hislam, J. and English, E. (2002) Pedagogical dilemmas in the National Literacy Strategy: primary teachers' perceptions, reflections and classroom behaviour, *Cambridge Journal of Education*, 32(1): 9–26.

Hodge, R. and Malcolm, I. (1981) *Communication and the Teacher*. Melbourne: Longman Cheshire.

Howe, A. (1992) *Making Talk Work*. London: Hodder and Stoughton.

Hughes, M. and Westgate, D. (1998) Possible enabling strategies in teacher-led talk with young pupils, *Language and Education*, 12(3): 174–91.

Hymes, D. (1972) On communicative competence, in J. Pride and J. Holmes (eds) *Sociolinguistics*. Harmondsworth: Penguin.

Kellogg, R.T. (1994) *The Psychology of Writing*. Oxford: Oxford University Press.

Kirby, P. (1996) Teacher questions during story-book readings: who's building whose building? *Reading*, 30(1): 8–15.

Lave, J. and Wenger, E. (1991) *Situated Learning: Legitimate Peripheral Participation*. Cambridge: Cambridge University Press.

Leat, D. and Lin, M. (2003) Developing a pedagogy of metacognition and transfer: some signposts for the generation and use of knowledge and the creation of research partnerships, *British Educational Research Journal*, 29(3): 383–415.

Many, J.E. (2002) An exhibition and analysis of verbal tapestries: understanding how scaffolding is woven into the fabric of instructional conversations, *Reading Research Quarterly*, 37(4): 376–407.

Maybin, J., Mercer, N. and Stierer, B. (1992) 'Scaffolding' learning in the classroom, in K. Norman (ed.) *Thinking Voices: the Work of the National Oracy Project*. London: Hodder and Stoughton.

Mercer, N. (1995) *The Guided Construction of Knowledge*. Clevedon: Multilingual Matters.

Mercer, N. (2000) *Words and Minds*. London: Routledge.

Moyles, J.R., Hargreaves, L.M. and Merry, R. (2001) *The Development of Primary Teachers' Understanding and Use of Interactive Teaching*. End of award report (ROOO 238200). Swindon: Economic and Social Research Council.

Mroz, M., Smith, F. and Hardman, F. (2000) The discourse of the Literacy Hour, *Cambridge Journal of Education*, 30(3): 379–90.

Myhill, D.A. (2003) Principled understanding? Teaching the active and passive voice, *Language and Education*, 17(5): 355–70.

Nutbrown, C. (1994) *Threads of Thinking*. London: Paul Chapman.

OECD (2002) Educational Research and Development in England, *OECD Review 2002*. Paris: OECD.

Office for Standards in Education (Ofsted) (2002) *The National Numeracy Strategy: The First Three Years 1999–2002*. London: Ofsted.

Palincsar, A. and Brown, A. (1984) Reciprocal teaching of comprehension-fostering and comprehension-monitoring activities, *Cognition and Instruction*, 1(2): 117–75.

Prestage, S., Perks, P. and Soares, A. (2003) Developing critical intelligence: tensions in the DfES model for Best Practice Research Scholarship, *Educational Review*, 55(1): 55–63.

Qualifications and Curriculum Authority (QCA) (2003) *New Perspectives on Spoken English in the Classroom*. London: QCA.

Qualifications and Curriculum Authority QCA (2004) *Introducing the Grammar of Talk*. London: QCA.

Reynolds, D. and Farrell, S. (1996) *World's Apart? A Review of International Surveys of Educational Achievement Involving England*. London: HMSO.

Rogoff, B. (1991) *Apprenticeship in Thinking*. New York: OUP.

Rowe, M.B. (1996) (reprinted from March 1969 issue) Science, silence, and sanctions, *Science and Children*, 34(1): 35–7.

Ryle, G. (1949) *The Concept of Mind*. London: Hutchinson's University Library.

Schön, D.A. (1990) *Educating the Reflective Practitioner: Toward a New Design for Teaching and Learning in the Profession*. San Francisco, CA: Jossey-Bass.

Sinclair, J.M. and Coulthard, M. (1975) *Towards an Analysis of Discourse: The Language of Teachers and Pupil*. London: Oxford University Press.

Skidmore, D. (2000) From pedagogical dialogue to dialogic pedagogy, *Language and Education*, 14(4): 283–96.

Summers, A. (1991) Unofficial stories in the classroom, *English in Education*, 25(2): 24–30.

Taber, K. (2002) 'Intense but it's all worth it in the end': the colearner's experience of the research process, *British Educational Research Journal*, 28(3): 435–57.

Tough, J. (1977) *The Development of Meaning*. New York: Wiley.

Valcke, M. (2002) Cognitive load: updating the theory? *Learning and Instruction*, 12(1): 147–54.

Vygotsky, L.S. (1986) *Thought and Language* (trans. A. Kozulin). Cambridge, MA: MIT Press.

Watts, M., Alsop, S., Gould, G, and Walsh, A. (1997) Prompting teachers' constructive reflection: pupils' questions as critical incidents, *International Journal of Science Education*, 19(9): 1025–37.

Webb, R. (1996) Changing primary classroom practice through teacher research, *Education 3 to 13*, 24(3): 18–26.

Wells, C.G. (1986) *The Meaning Makers: Children Learning Language and Using Language to Learn*. London: Hodder and Stoughton Educational.

Wells, C.G. (1999) *Dialogic Inquiry. Toward a Sociocultural Practice and Theory of Education*. Cambridge: Cambridge University Press.

Wood, D. (1988) *How Children Think and Learn*. Oxford: Basil Blackwell.

Wragg, E.C and Brown, G. (2001a) *Explaining in the Primary School*. London: RoutledgeFalmer.

Wragg, E.C. and Brown, G. (2001b) *Questioning in the Primary School*. London: RoutledgeFalmer.

Bibliography

Burns, C. and Myhill, D. (2004) Inactive or interactive? *Cambridge Journal of Education*, 34(1): 35–49.

Department for Education and Employment (DfEE) (1999) *Engaging all Pupils*. London: DfEE.

Eisner, E.W. (1996) *Cognition and Curriculum Reconsidered*. London: Paul Chapman.

Flanagan, J.C. (1954) The Critical Incident Technique, *Psychological Bulletin*, 51(4): 327–58.

Flanders, N. (1970) *Analyzing Teaching Behavior*. London: Addison Wesley.

Gall, M.D. (1970) The use of questioning in teaching, *Review of Educational Research*, 40: 707–21.

Galton, M., Simon, B. and Croll, P. (1980) *Inside the Primary Classroom*. London: Routledge and Kegan Paul.

Geekie, P., Cambourne, B. and Fitzsimmons, P. (1999) *Understanding Literacy Development*. Stoke-on-Trent: Trentham Books.

Haworth, A. (2001) The Re-positioning of Oracy: a millennium project? *Cambridge Journal of Education*, 31(1): 11–23.

Haworth, A. (1999) Bakhtin in the Classroom: What constitutes a dialogic text? Some lessons from small group interaction, *Language and Education*, 13(2): 99–117.

Heath, S. (1983) *Ways with Words: Language, Life and Work in Communities and Classrooms*. Cambridge: Cambridge University Press.

Hilton, M. (2001) Writing process and progress: Where do we go from here? *English in Education*, 35(1): 4–11.

Hilton, M. (2002) Intricate complexities, *English in Education*, 36(1): 1–4.

Hilton, M. and Anderson, H. (1997) Speaking subjects: the development of a conceptual framework, *English in Education*, 31(1): 12–23.

Kirschner, P.A. (2002) Cognitive load theory: implications of cognitive load theory on the design of learning, *Learning and Instruction*, 12(1): 1–10.

Martin, N. (1975) *Understanding Children Talking*. Harmondsworth: Penguin.

Myhill, D.A. and Dunkin, F. (2002) That's a good question, *Literacy Today*, 33: 8–9.

Myhill, D.A. (2002) Bad boys and good girls? Patterns of interaction and response in whole class teaching, *British Educational Research Journal*, 28(3): 339–52.

Myhill, D.A. (2003) Principled understanding? Teaching the active and passive voice, *Language and Education*, 17(5): 355–70.

Myhill, D.A. and Brackley, M. (2004) Making connections: Teacher's use of children's prior knowledge in whole class discourse, *British Journal of Educational Studies*, 52(3): 263–75.

Newbolt, H.J. (1921) *The Teaching of English in England*. London: HMSO.

Norman K. (ed.) (1992) *Thinking Voices: the Work of the National Oracy Project*. London: Hodder and Stoughton.

Scarth, J. and Hammersley, M. (1986) Questioning ORACLE: an assessment of ORACLE's analysis of teachers' questions, *Educational Research*, 28(3): 174–83.

Sweller, J. (1994) Cognitive load theory, learning difficulty and instructional design, *Learning and Instruction*, 4(4): 295–312.

Tannen, D. (1993) What's in a frame? Surface evidence for underlying expectations, in D. Tannen (ed.) *Framing in Discourse*. Oxford: Oxford University Press.

Teacher Training Agency (TTA) (2002) *Qualifying to Teach*. London: TTA.

Weis, L. (1990) *Working Class without Work*. New York: Routledge.

Wilkinson, A. (1966) *Spoken English*. Birmingham: University of Birmingham.

Wood, D. (1992) Teaching talk: How modes of teacher talk affect pupil participation, in K. Norman (ed.) *Thinking Voices: the Work of the National Oracy Project*. London: Hodder and Stoughton.

Wood, D. and Wood, H. (1988) Questioning versus student initiative, in J.T. Dillon (ed.) *Questioning and Discussion*. Norwood: New Jersey, Ablex Publishing Corporation.

Wragg, E.C. (1993) *Primary Teaching Skills*. London: Routledge.

Index

Related books from Open University Press

Purchase from www.openup.co.uk or order through your local bookseller

LEARNING WITHOUT LIMITS

Susan Hart, Annabelle Dixon, Mary Jane Drummond and Donald McIntyre

- Why do some teachers insist on teaching without recourse to judgements about ability?
- What are the key principles on which they draw as they organize and provide for learning?
- What is the significance of their alternative approach for classrooms in the 21st century?

This book explores ways of teaching that are free from determinist beliefs about ability. In a detailed critique of the practices of ability labelling and ability focused teaching, *Learning without Limits* examines the damage these practices can do to young people, teachers and the curriculum.

Drawing on a research project at the University of Cambridge, the book features nine vivid case studies (from Year 1 to Year 11) that describe how teachers have developed alternative practices despite considerable pressure on them and on their schools and classrooms. The authors analyse these case studies and identify the key concept of transformability as a distinguishing feature of these teachers' approach. They construct a model of pedagogy based on transformability: the mind-set that children's futures as learners are not predetermined, and that teachers can help to strengthen and ultimately transform young people's capacity to learn through the choices they make. The book shows how transformability-based teaching can play a central role in constructing an alternative improvement agenda.

This book will inspire teachers, student teachers, lecturers and policy makers, as well as everyone who has a stake in how contemporary education and practice affect children's future lives and life chances.

Contents
Part one: The problem in context – Why learning without limits? – What's wrong with ability labelling? – Researching teachers' thinking and practices – Part two: The case studies – nine teachers in action – Part three: Towards an alternative model – The principle of transformability – From principle to practice – The contexts of teaching for learning without limits – Pupils' perspectives on learning without limits – An alternative improvement agenda – Conclusion – Index.

192pp   0 335 21259 X (Paperback)   0 335 21260 3 (Hardback)